"This book shows you how
determine the course of you.

Brian Tracy - Author- How the Best Leaders Lead)

"I first had the pleasure of meeting Ramzi Karim at a Branding Boot Camp that I was facilitating in the Toronto area in 2009. Ramzi was brimming with confidence as he articulated his passion for publishing his new book. I have had the pleasure of inspiring Ramzi to action and more importantly reviewing his stellar book. Ramzi has crafted an excellent prescription recruiting top talent. Ramzi's approach to interviewing is intelligent, well thought out and logical. I want to congratulate Ramzi for being the **FIRST** to put a coherent step by step process together that can be easily followed.

Ramzi is an articulate communicator and successful at presenting the key principles that prepare you for an interview. Every principle resonates with supporting rational so the reader has an insight into their prospective employers mind.

This book is for anyone wanting to kick start or advance their career. Ramzi's 'street smart' principle to winning over your prospective employer is an intelligent and savvy approach.

I would highly recommend organizations and individuals to carefully follow Ramzi's principles."

Gerry Visca - International Speaker - Canada's Creative Coach
www.gerryvisca.com

"A common sense approach to the interview process. Whether you are entering the work force for the first time or starting out again, practical and common sense advice to guide you through what could otherwise be an intimidating experience."

Sue Z – Sales Manager

"You must read this book; it will make your life much easier and gives you all the answers you need in your search for a job"

"An extremely insightful look into the interviewing process. Helps you to understand what the interviewer is looking for and what they are judging you on."

"This book is not just a valuable resource for the job seeker but also valuable for recruiting managers to help them hire suitable candidates."

"I always had difficulties in an interview when asked *what are your weaknesses?* Reading this book gave me the perfect answer, thank you"

"Finally a book focusing not just on winning interviews but also on how to survive your first ninety days at a new job."

"As a parent it gave me extremely valuable tools on how to help and coach my children to succeed on their interviews."

HOW TO MASTER THE ART OF INTERVIEWING

ALL YOU NEED TO KNOW TO INCREASE YOUR HIRE POWER

Ramzi Karim

authorHOUSE®

AuthorHouse™
1663 Liberty Drive
Bloomington, IN 47403
www.authorhouse.com
Phone: 1-800-839-8640

First published by AuthorHouse 2/1/2010

ISBN: 978-1-4490-0703-4 (sc)
ISBN: 978-1-4490-0705-8 (e)
ISBN: 978-1-4490-0704-1 (hc)

Library of Congress Control Number: 2010900958

Printed in the United States of America
Bloomington, Indiana

This book is printed on acid-free paper.

CONTENTS

Introduction   Why Write This Book   vii

Chapter 1   Why we interview- What are we looking for?   1

Chapter 2   Getting Started   15

Chapter 3   Where to Begin   29

Chapter 4   Interview formats   65

Chapter 5   How to Prepare For the Interview   81

Chapter 6   Answering Questions during Interview   97

Chapter 7   Referencing   115

Chapter 8   Body Language   123

Chapter 9   Thirty Common Interview Questions
            and Answers   137

Chapter 10 How to survive your First 90 days in a Job   159

Chapter 11 Advice to Parents   179

Chapter 12 Putting it All Together   195

INTRODUCTION

WHY WRITE THIS BOOK

A warm welcome to all those who are taking a sneak pick view into this book on Interview. This is not just a book on the development of interview skills. Rather, this is a miracureall (an all out solution) to the intricacies that you need to prepare yourself for, before facing an interview. It has been a goal and dream of mine to be able to share my experiences with job seekers who have just started to look for work, or who had lost their jobs and are struggling to find a new one.

What I truly wish to accomplish through this book is- to be able to help and serve those deserving souls, who are fighting with a commendable die –hard attitude in order to land them an opportunity of a suitable job. Through this book, I wish to guide all those job aspirants who may be high school students, young graduates, mid term career changers, professionals venturing for a new and better opportunity, as well as all those chair holders of organizations, who need to gear themselves up before they actually come face to face with an interviewer or an interviewee. This book will also cater to serve all those who have suddenly found themselves in a jobless situation as an outcome of this economic mayhem and are in a process to grab one as soon as possible. I strongly feel that this book would attract most of you for this fascinating fact that, it serves the purpose of a varied camp of job aspirants. So, if you reading this book, congratulations!!

You are on your way towards a better job learning how to prepare and handle interviews. You will also acquire the techniques of reducing your fear, and increasing your confidence when you step into the arena.

This book is a perfect compilation of some sure fire success secrets that would maximize you prospects in the job market. Not only that, it would end up landing you a dream job that you have always aspired for. If you are wondering how, simply explore through the book. The book will instruct you how to look for a better job, how to curb the inhibitions, how to plan up and prepare for an interview, how to boost up confidence in your being. As you cruise through the pages of this book, I am sure you would start feeling the strong positive vibes within you through the life changing education that it imparts.

You may have read other books about interviewing, which are mainly written from theoretical point of views. These have been mostly written by professionals who might not have conducted an interview in their live time or faced one except when they might have been looking for job themselves.

This book would definitely be more beneficial to you all as it is written off with a practical approach, by someone who has been involved in the process of interviewing candidates for decades! For the last 20 years I have been in this business and have conducted over 5,000 interviews. I have spent around 3000 hours in the process of screening potential candidates. I have dealt with good candidates as well as bad ones, being an integral part of the entire process of interview. I have seen many instances where deserving candidates could not bag the job because of poor preparation. I have also seen many good or bad examples of behaviors that had made candidates successful or unsuccessful in landing a job.

All the facts laid in the pages of the book are based on proven theories. So they are much more valuable. Through this book you can teach your self how to put together your available resources and make your job –hunt comparatively easier.

If you still have some doubts concerning the content in this book that makes it stand apart from the other books written on the same subject, I would love to throw light upon this so that you get its implication in your career.

I presume all of you who are now flipping through the pages of this book, are aware of the simple fact that finding a job for yourself is not at all an easy proposition. It is not something you can trifle with. As a matter of fact, the job of job searching is a high –end stressful affair. May be you have been subjected to a situation where you have been trying hard, and are continually giving your best –but in vain. Your persistent efforts in job searching have still not been fruitful in landing that job that you were desperately looking for. At times this stress takes a toll on your mind and soul. This could be fatal as it could lead you to a serious state of depression. Once you are exposed to this state you would surely end up loosing a lot of prospects. So don't let it be your case.

The exact problem that you might be facing is that, you are putting in your best effort; but it is not yielding result due to lack of following a proper, systematic way that you should go. This might happen as you may not be technically sound of the methods that you need to follow. You need to follow up proper modes of actions and methods. You need to channelise your thoughts properly. This book will be your soul mate in your crusade against your present state of unemployment.

This book, will give the readers the know how of facing an interview from start to finish, and about how to successfully get a job. It will also guide you on what you need to do once you have landed the job successfully, in order to compete successfully in a competitive work place. I had my two teenage daughters get their first jobs during high school by applying to only one place, and landing the job after their first interview due to my coaching. I felt extremely proud when they informed me that after following my advice it was like a piece of cake act for them to face the interview and crack it successfully.

The reason behind citing this example was that I would like to claim whoever follows the rules laid in this book would not find it hard at all to perform much better in any sort of interviews that he she has to face in future.

Let me assure you of one thing. While you are reading or working with this book, you will surely undergo a process of transformation in your entire personality. If you are too nervous about facing the interview board or any kind of technical interview I would suggest that before making your move to the interview venue, do not fail to take a very close view at the contents of the book. I am sure you will unearth a spring of spontaneous inspiration within yourself. After making a thorough and detailed reading of the content of the book you can surely unhinge the hidden potentials and latent qualities that lay dormant in your self, of which may be you were also not fully aware of.

This book will provide proven and practical ways on how to land a job easily and make the process much easier. It will lift the pressure off from those who are reluctant in finding a job due to lack of confidence, experience or set backs, and encourage them to take positive action. Thus they will be successfully driven on the path of their career. This book will also help all those job hunters who have become victim due to the cost cutting mechanisms followed by companies, in order to combat the terrible impact of recession on the economy.

In my years of experience as an employment seeker and employment provider, I have read many books and articles about interviewing. However I could not find a book that combines interviews and other qualities like attitude and motivation, with practical helps that paint the picture for you. I could not lay my hand on a book like this that would   make me think and help to succeed when I got a position.

Therefore, this is more than just a book. It's your instant assessor in terms of bringing out the most subtle qualities, as well as providing you with all the required level of confidence with which you can easily and definitely crack the interview.

The most appealing part of the book does not restrict its functions to unearthing the subtle secrets of the art of interviewing only. Rather, it takes good care of certain other facets which are equally crucial. I have incorporated certain facts that would be regarded as prerequisite parts of your personality whether you are a fresher out for a job hunt, or a student looking for a part time job or a mid career employee who is out of the job and on a frantic search for another deserving one.

The facts that I am talking about are time management, which is supposed to be a must no matter whatever field you choose to be; drafting a proper Resume, as an effective resume makes you salable for a company; cover letters, that tends to offer your Resume a good back up that it needs; and obviously an insight into the subtle art of preparation for the interview. Take moving for an interview as a battle. Focus only on the win. As every battle asks for the warriors to be geared up for the hostilities of war, so is the case with an interview. You need to prepare well for all oddities of the interview process and that's what this book does. It fully prepares you for the ultimate battle.

When you are inside the interview chamber you have to answer a lot of intriguing questions. Some might be flat but most of them would be technical, related to your field. There could be interpersonal questionnaire to judge what kind of a human being you actually are. Here, your I.Q level would also be put to test.

Therefore, Interviewers will accordingly select questions. In such situations you need to bounce back with an appropriate answer to each of these questions. This book aids you in mastering the subtle art of responding perfectly to these intricate questions without coming out of your comfort zone. With a little bit of practice you can master all the required traits of this art. So if you had been an innocent victim of this economic mayhem, and had to kiss your job good bye, I would say there is absolutely no reason to feel low as if you are being pushed to the corner. Whatever your condition may be, my book will help you to tackle the gravest of all situations by landing you another job opportunity.

In the frame of this book you would get an excellent guide who will instruct you on how to successfully get a job and what exactly you need to do once you have bagged the job in order to keep your existence alive in this competitive market. So my responsibility towards you does not come to an end just by landing you a job it comes to a full circle after getting you established in a job.

The reason that chiefly works behind the publication of this book is, a sense of duty to share my experiences with all those who seek job ardently. As I had not been offered a book that covered every aspect of dealing with an interview and landing a job, I had decided to put in all my experience and expertise in this field to create a healthy package for you. If this package of interview skills combined with other qualities like motivational skills, attitude and other practical guides and helps you to secure your future, I would deem my purpose to be fulfilled.

I am truly looking for your feedback about this book and welcome your ideas and suggestion. Please drop me a line at- **rik@rogers. com**

Good Luck!!

CHAPTER 1

WHY WE INTERVIEW- WHAT ARE WE LOOKING FOR?

"Your future depends on many things but mostly yourself."~ Frank Tyger

A candidate in order to do well in an interview must understand why we interview and what we are looking for. The interview process concerns meeting with a lot of strangers, and selecting within a very short period of time, the right candidate for a position.

When we interview, we make judgments on candidates, based on the facts available on their résumés. And what do we try to judge? We try to judge the current performance of the candidate, the future prediction, and whether they will fit into the culture of the organization. When we select a candidate, it is like starting a new relationship. We all hope that this relationship based on mutual respect, high expectation and ethical behavior will be long lasting. If the relationship faces termination, we would expect that it will have a respectful and dignified ending so as to protect the interest of both the parties. To a recruiter, bad selection of a candidate costs a great deal of money, wastes resources, and disrupts the business.

Interviewing is a necessary and perhaps the only way to select a candidate. That is why the process of selection begins with its focus on fact finding. We search for key qualities and attributes that one must have, in order to be successful in any work environment. I have put some of these key qualities into a simple formula which is easy to remember.

If you look at a job description, you will notice that these key qualities have been mentioned time and again. The more you understand these qualities and prepare for the questions to come, the better success you will have. Simple preparation will increase your chances of a better interview and give you an edge over the more experienced or qualified candidates; the result- you getting the job.

F A C E C I A: The Key Qualities Needed for Succeeding in Interviews

The acronym FACECIA will provide you with a key to the essential attributes needed by an interviewee to succeed in an interview. The acronym FACECIA provides a deep insight into those vitals traits on the basis of which the interviewer would judge you. These key aspects of an interviewee that would make or break the interview process are as follows:

- Facts

- Attitude

- Confidence

- Experience

- Communication Skills

- Interpersonal Skills

- Analytical Skills

Facts

During the interview your interviewer will try to find the facts about your background. These facts will represent an overall picture of you and will sum up your experiences, your character, and personality. Always be sure to get your facts straight.

The interviewer being a virtual stranger to you would obviously try to form an overall idea about you through the facts provided to him on your résumé. He will peruse through your experience certificates and academic credentials and try to verify the facts provided to him. That's why, it is all the more important that whatever information you provide to your interviewer, must be 100% true. Being Complacent is a cardinal sin for an interviewee. Even if you have the adequate experience and educational qualification to qualify for a job, then also you should never get complacent. Whatever facts and figures you provide to your interviewer, you should mentally prepare yourself to be challenged about those facts. You must be able to explain any gaps between any schools that you attended or any job changes.

For example, if you finished high school in 2004 and attended university in 2006, you must be able to explain a logical reason for the gap. What experiences did you gain during that period and how it made you better prepared for university? Similarly, if there is a gap between your total employment years, you must be able to explain the gaps and give accurate reasons for them.

It's inevitable that you would feel unsure and defensive, if you are grilled about the facts presented in your resume. If you have a gap between your employment years you should mentally prepare yourself for such questions as- "So, what was happening from July 2002 through September 2002?" Don't panic over any questions asked about the phase of temporary unemployment in your career.

If you were truly unemployed during a period in your career, you should try to keep your explanation about that temporary unemployment succinct and factual. You should endeavor to highlight the positive things that you learnt and did within that period, and gradually try to steer the conversation back to your qualifications and interest in the job for which you are being interviewed.

Thus, prior to an interview try to work with the facts of the resume gap, and craft a 2-3 sentence response to an anticipated inquiry. Your response needs to be honest, yet it does not need to include all of the convoluted details or the background stories.

The same theory applies to any gap that you might have had in your academic career. If you had left your studies midway due to any pressing personal issue and then resumed it later, you should be truthful about it. But try to present the details in such a way that you are not left looking too capricious and fickle minded.

Attitude

The interviewer will want to find out about your attitude towards work. He or she will want to determine your reasons for applying for a particular job. He will want to know how many places you have applied for already. Are they all over the place, or are they specific and targeted at their areas of expertise. For example, if someone applied for a sales position, during the interview it would become evident that in reality they do not like sales, but would rather prefer to do a clerical job. This would reveal that the person doesn't have the right attitude towards sales, and as a result may not be selected for the position that he/she had applied for.

Thus, your attitude, towards the job you have applied for, would give your interviewer an idea about your propensity and competency towards it. You might have enough educational qualification to apply for a particular job, but if you don't have the right kind of attitude required for the job you would never be able to excel in it. Your interviewer would try to find out whether you have the right frame of mind to reach the zenith in the job that you have applied for. That is why you should ensure that you possess the right kind of attitude and a positive frame of mind before you venture out to give an interview.

Your interviewer would judge your attitude on various criterions. Some of the other facets of having the right kind of attitude for a job have been discussed below.

A) Positive Attitude: Are you a Positive Thinker? Do you talk negatively about your experiences from your previous colleagues and supervisors? When faced with problems, do you think of it as an opportunity to learn, or do you see it as an obstacle. Positive thoughts shape our moods and create positive energy. On the other hand, negative thoughts create depression and a pessimistic outlook towards work, and life in general.

An interview is a process of selling yourself. So, if you don't realize your true potential your interviewer would never be able to appreciate your true qualities. Thus, a positive attitude is the best thing you can bring along with yourself to a job interview. When you think positively about yourself and what you have to offer, your interviewer would also recognize this and would want to learn more about you.

You should always remember that you are your strongest asset. Try to harp on your strong points and capabilities as much as possible during an interview. But, at the same time, be prepared to answer questions about your weaknesses too. You should endeavor to make your weaknesses work for you by rehearsing a response about the harmless nature of your weakness, and the plans that you have made to overcome it. The interviewer will surely be impressed at your ability to comprehend and deal with your shortcomings.

The act of writing out your answers to difficult interview questions, particularly if you have a glitch in your resume or background, is a great way to sound positive.

B) Self Motivation: Are you a Self-motivator? It is hard to motivate someone who is not self motivated. Your interviewer will want to find out what kind of initiatives you have taken in your current or previous job and what kind of extracurricular activities you were involved in.

Do you set goals and have you achieved them? What have you learned from setting these goals? Your interviewer wants to find out, if you motivate yourself, or do you always rely on someone else to motivate you and guide you.

One common question that an interviewer asks is, "In your résumé you wrote that you are self-motivated; give me an example of this and what was its impact on you and your team?" It is important that when you are faced with such a question that you have a few good examples of situations that proves that you are indeed a self motivator. What if in fact you are not a self motivator?

The best way to answer this sort of question is to express your willingness to take initiative when it comes to additional work. You should always try to emphasize your interest in increasing your knowledge and contacts. Your answers should prove to your interviewer that you can self-motivate by setting ambitious goals, working hard, and keeping up with current trends.

Try to prepare yourself in advance for this kind of questions from your interviewer. You can rehearse an answer for this kind of a question prior to the interview. Prepare and answer in advance which won't be too elaborate and boring and yet be satisfactory enough to your interviewer. Try to brainstorm about possible interview questions on your attitude and come up with thoughtful answers to them. This is an advice which is applicable for other kind of interview questions too.

Confidence:

The interviewer will be looking for a self-confident   person. Do you quit easily or are you unstoppable? Perception is reality- the more confident the person comes across, the most likelihood that they will succeed. The way one judges self confidence is through their handshake, eye contact and the way they are dressed up. The interviewer will be observing whether you are smiling and enthusiastic, and if you talk about your achievements with a clear voice.

A handshake with the interviewer is the first personal contact that you make with him. So make sure that you give him or her firm, not bone-crushing handshake. While you are shaking your interviewer's hand try to keep direct eye contact to exude confidence.

Whether you are sitting or standing, make sure that your posture portrays your inner confidence. Try to sit properly during the interview and avoid nervous habits like fidgeting, smoking or chewing gums during the interview because that might send wrong signals to your interviewer. Your demeanor and confident attitude can positively influence your interview results to a great extent.

Your Dress attitude, tone of voice, and mannerisms all create a positive impression. An interviewer uses these impressions to judge you on your level of confidence. A confident attitude and visual impression are equally important as the things you say during your interview.

If you feel that you lack in self-confidence, the best way to build your self-confidence is to focus on the areas that you are strong in and good at. Again do your home work; and come to the interview prepared. Do not procrastinate and put things off until the last minute. The best way to boost your self confidence is to be totally prepared for the interview. To augment your chances of getting hired, you need to do some research with regard to the company. You can log on to the website of your prospective employers and check what they are looking for.

Gleaning an array of information about the company will help you answer the interviewer's questions with confidence. Once you get to know what the company is looking for, you can be confident enough to elaborate on your own experience with respect to what they are seeking.

Experience

The way you market yourself and your experience, will make a big difference in getting the job. Experience carries big value when it comes to selecting the right candidate. That is why the majority of recruitment advertisements list some key experience as a prerequisite to qualify for the job.

If you don't have enough experience, this does not mean you should not apply for the job either, it will not be the final consideration in the selection of a candidate.

When you lack certain experiences, focus on building your transferable skills. For example, if you are a home maker and trying to re-enter the job market, focus on what you have learned from raising up kids, for example the ability to multi-task, to be flexible, organized, handle criticism well, and handle adversity and conflict well.

If you are a student who has had very little work experience, then you can draw your examples from other experiences of life. Your school record and community activities can be valuable attestations to your abilities. You can use these valuable experiences in addition to the references work experience that you have made.

Prepare your own transferable skills and try to match it with the job posting with real examples on how well prepared you are for this job. Even before you go for the interview, try to thoroughly read through the job description more than once. Try to zero on the mission statement of your prospective employers. If it is full of teambuilding jargon, then during your interview you must emphasize your past experiences of working with teams.

You should know how to communicate the key skills and relevant experience that your interviewer is looking for in candidates. It's all about highlighting the skills that land jobs. For example, if a job description states that the company is looking for a candidate with management skills and juggling multiple projects, then you could utilize this information to your advantage by highlighting those past experiences which required such qualities. You can outline how you single-handedly coordinated a sales meeting of more than hundred employees of your former company, with only two months notice.

While you speak about your past experience of working in other organization, you should never commit the cardinal mistake of criticizing them or badmouthing them. It is essential for you to speak positively about former experiences. Even if your former employer had been grumpy and ill-tempered, never complain about a previous employer. You should always try to find something positive in every former work experience and emphasize that.

Communication Skills

Communication skills can be both verbal and non-verbal. In this section we will focus on verbal communication skills. Non-verbal skills will be covered in a separate chapter to follow. Your interviewer will want to find out how effectively you can verbally communicate the contents of your résumé. To help you communicate effectively, make sure you speak clearly and concisely. Try to avoid big words and jargons, avoid smart Alec comments, jokes etc. And remember, whatever you do, do not argue with the interviewer even if they push your buttons. This is a sure way to test your temper and emotions. Also, if you don't understand a question, ask the interviewer to repeat it. If the question is unclear, try to paraphrase it.

The second part of verbal communication skills, which the interviewer is looking for and judging on, is your listening skills. This is critical in the job interview. It brings out to the interviewer, your ability to comprehend complex questions, how you respond and articulate your answers and whether you are feeling comfortable or hesitant with your responses.

Glossophobia, the fear of public speaking, is the number one fear in America, which troubles many business professionals. However, in order to make an impact in your professional field you require refined communication skills. If you fail to communicate your ideas to others effectively, you may not come across as a very confident communicator. As a result, you will never climb up the corporate ladder or might even lose business deals. That is the precise reason why many interviewers place immense importance on the good communication skills of their interviewees.

One of the best ways you can achieve your goal of impressing your employer with your communication skills is by proficiently communicating your enthusiasm for your prospective job. You should express your avid enthusiasm for the position component, and if you are able to play this role effectively, you should get an offer of employment.

Enthusiasm can be pretty infectious and it can even determine a tie-breaker between you and another interviewee. If you are honest and deft in expressing your enthusiasm about working conditions of the organization and your ability to be successful, the interviewer will be feeling enthusiastic about you too. If two people who have similar credentials are being interviewed, it is often the one who can express his passion and interest about the job that gets chosen. You have to communicate correctly why you have chosen to apply for this job. The bottom line is that you have to impress your employer with your skill of persuasion.

However, don't go overboard trying to impress your interviewer with your verbal communication skills. You might misinterpret the questions being asked so it's important to listen carefully to what is being asked before you answer a question. Whatever points you put forward on your behalf they should all be lucid and coherent.

Don't be afraid to ask for clarification if you don't understand a question. It will be much more embarrassing to speculate about the question and give an inappropriate answer. Remember that, communication skills not only means impressing your prospective employer with your gift of gab, communication skill also refers to your ability of communicating your thoughts and ideas to your interviewer, and at the same time your promptness in understanding his ideas.

The listening skills that you reveal during an interview are essential to your success as an interview candidate. To improve your listening skills, stay calm, don't be nervous, don't get sidetracked or lose focus. Stay motivated, and focus on your goal to impress you interviewer. You should set small goals to impress your employer with your communication skill.

Interpersonal Skills

When it comes to interpersonal skills during an interview, the interviewer is trying to find out if you can get along well with coworkers, classmates, teachers, managers, and people of power and authority. He wants to find out how you deal with people you dislike or disagree with. Do you take things personally? How do you handle criticism? How do you resolve conflict? How do you handle pressure?

To understand your level of interpersonal skills, you need to know how your behavior and feelings which exist inside you, influences your interactions with others.

To develop one's interpersonal skills, you need to:

- Smile and put on a happy face so people don't perceive you as grumpy, mean, miserable or unapproachable.

- Don't complain; nobody wants to listen to people who complain, blame others and constantly whine.

- Get involved; don't shy away from groups, participate in committees, volunteer, pay attention to what is going on around you and genuinely compliment and appreciate others.

It would be a prudent gesture on your part to prepare a list of examples in which you were part of a successful team effort. This would testify to your positive interpersonal skills. These examples of your brilliant team effort might not be on your resume, but your interviewer might coax you to give such examples. If it is possible, in the course of your conversation with your interviewer, try to reflect back on incidents where you coordinated a team effort. It is sufficient enough to provide examples of your experience of working well in a group, but it is even better if you can show that you can also lead and take charge of a group.

You should not be afraid to mention troubles, some minor troubles that you faced while handling a team. But be sure to mention how you could overcome that trouble too. It is quite obvious that a group of people cannot agree all the time; if you can display your ability to work through problems and succeed to your interviewer that would have a paramount on your selection for that job.

However, if your interviewer asks you questions about your past relationships with colleagues and managers make sure you site positive examples. The reason is, even though your interviewer seems sympathetic he is really not going to be interested in complaints. This will give the interviewer an impression of you being a complainer and who wants to hire a chronic complainer.

Analytical Skills

Many job descriptions state analytical skills as a prerequisite for the job. The interviewer is interested in finding out- how you constantly separate fact from fiction? How do you tackle problems? How do you break the problem into its most basic elements? Is your manner of thinking rational and objective? Do you follow a positive and logical course of action?

Some of the questions that you can expect would be like:

- What kind of difficulties have you had with work task and how did you find a way to rectify the problem and work more efficiently?

- What reason and logic were used to resolve a problem?

- Are you a problem solver or do you depend on others to solve it?

To improve your analytical skill you need to:

- Improve your observation skills. Try to understand what the causes of the problem are, how many factors cause a particular problem.

- Analyze the Results. Find how the results are obtained, break it down to groups and sub groups. How results in one area affect results on another area?

- Find out the cause. Once you have the results, find out what the causes of the problem are. What factors are impacting your analysis?

- Come up with a solution. Put the pieces together like a jigsaw puzzle.

- Share your solution. Sharing your solution gains you respect and leadership. It will also get people to perceive you as a solution provider for problems.

Thus, the bottom-line is that no employer wants a mindless drone for an employee. That is why analytical skill should be an important part of any interviewee repertoire. You have to remember that the interviewer doesn't want you to parrot some bookish lines but rather they want you to think on your feet and respond promptly on trying situations. You should understand that they are trying to hire those problem solvers who have enough determination and willpower, not to tug at their sleeves at every drop of a hat. That is why it is critical to make your interviewer understand that you can understand and resolve a difficult situation better than the other candidates and can come through in the clutch.

CHAPTER 2

GETTING STARTED

"It's the little things you do that can make a big difference. What are you attempting to accomplish? What little thing can you do today that will make you more effective? You are probably only one step away from greatness."
~ Bob Proctor

When does the hiring process start?

The hiring process actually starts when you go into an establishment and hand in your resume or pick up an employment application.

First impressions are everything. The way you look, the way you dress and the way you interact or communicate when you hand in your resume or application actually influences the mind of the employer without you realizing it.

How is that possible?

In the first place, the business world is an extremely competitive world and there are many candidates applying for the same position.

Secondly everyone is strapped for time with limited resources for the interview. The interview process is actually very costly for employers, especially since some employers conduct up to three interviews before they can decide on candidates. The cost includes advertising, printing materials, time spent for interviewing and referencing. All this costs the productivity of the employer, who has to take time out of the numerous other responsibilities that he has to carry out in his prescheduled work list in his fast paced workplace.

What happens when you walk into an establishment looking scurfy, wearing torn pants, too many visible piercing, with visible tattoos, or chewing gum, or accompanied by friends who do not look presentable? The chances of you, getting an interview is very unlikely; specially, if five people already had applied for the same position, and have walked in well dressed, well groomed, with a better presentation of themselves.

Try to remember that first impressions are vital in a job scenario. If you are not impeccably groomed, and present yourself too casually dressed while you go to pick up an application form, people might deem you as irresponsible or too lackadaisical about your job prospects. This is surely not the impression you would like to give to your prospective employers.

Many companies instruct their front line employees to screen people who are applying for employment and make note on first impressions. You could be screened out or eliminated even before you had handed in your application, if you are not properly groomed.

What should you do then?

Here are a few practical advices as to what you need to do before you send in your application to a potential employer:

1. Pre-visit the Premises at least once:

During your visit observe the environment and the staff. Look for common trends in the appearance of the employees. Look at the way they are dressed up. Observe the hair styles and notice if there is visible piercing or tattoos. This will tell you if this place is tolerant of certain things. Notice if associates are wearing uniform.

Imagine yourself in the uniform and see if you like it. Do you fit that environment? When you finish your observation and you think that this is the place you would like to work, ask for application only if you are dressed appropriately and groomed to the standard of that work place.

If you are not dressed appropriately or you are with friends who are not dressed and groomed properly, then leave the place. Come back at a later date for a second visit dressed properly to pick up an application form. How you will fill up the application and hand it in, we will talk more about that later on.

2. Introduce yourself to a Manager or Supervisor:

During your visit at the office premises of your prospective employers, you can seek out the manager and supervisor of that premises, and find out if they are hiring. Make sure you shake their hands with a big smile on your face. Congenial and politeness would always add an extra edge to your efforts. Ask what positions are available. Sometimes some position become open and the employer may not have had a chance to put a sign for hiring or advertising it yet.

Even if they do not have any openings which are appropriate for your skill-set, they would remember your face and enthusiasm when one is available. This will give you chance to get a better feel for your niche field and also give a chance for the company to get to know you.

So, if you want to get hired by a company of esteem, you have to be proactive. It's up to you to find out about the job positions which are open. And for this, you need to put in some effort. Try to be polite and graceful even while enquiring about open vacancies from the managers or the supervisor of the company unit you are visiting. If you display any kind of brash behavior and over confident mannerism, chances are that you might not even coax out the information about the positions which have not been advertised yet.

3. Get the Person's Name or Business card

This will make it easy for you when you apply. In your cover letter, you should address the person by name and remind them that you enjoyed talking with them and why you would like to work at this place.

This approach applies a personal touch to your application letter. It emphasizes the fact that you have been diligent enough to visit the company premises before you chose to apply for a job in that company. This gesture would serve to underscore your sincerity and dedication towards your job.

Apart from this when you mention the person's name in your application letter you make optimum use of the contact you have already created with the company. If you are lucky enough, the manager or supervisor you have already spoken to might remember you and provide some positive inputs about you.

4. Enquire on their Employment Criterion

You can always ask the manager or supervisor of that office a couple of questions on their most sought out qualities in an employee. Whatever information you might glean from the supervisor or manager of that company, it would provide you with some extra advantage during your interview. This information might act as vital clues about how to conduct your behavior during the interview or what exactly the company is looking for in their employees. It would also help you to read between the lines of the job description that you would be provided.

Don't over do anything. The person might not have time to talk to you for long and you should take care to see that you do not present yourself as a pushy person. The subtle approach always pays in this regard. You have to strike the right balance between being pushy and inquisitive. If you are deemed as being too pushy then it might hamper your job prospects in the long run. It's no use trying to go over board in your enthusiasm and irritating your first contact person.

5. Talk with the Employees

If possible, seek an opportunity to talk to a couple of employees and see how they like working at the establishment, and try to identify some of the things which are important to the company.

Even more than the supervisors and the manager, these employees having hands-on experience of knowing the nitty-gritty's of the company would be able to provide you with some vital inside info on the company. If you are lucky enough, you might even find the names of the probable person who might be interviewing you. This might later help you to glean more information about them and prepare yourself for the interview.

However, while talking with the employees of your company you plan to work in future, you should follow the same principle of covert enthusiasm. You should remember not to be overzealous in this regard and irritate the employees you have been trying to coax that information from. Any kind of serious grilling might have a boomerang effect and reduce your chances of getting hired.

6. Observe the Place

If it is a retail environment, watch the customers; see if they are getting helped. Observe the attitude of the employees they have; whether they are friendly to the customers, how does the merchandizing looks like, whether the place is clean, check out where the washrooms are, etc. This is a secret that you all should know- the maintenance of the washrooms tells you a lot about the place. It tells you whether they care about the customer, as well as reflects the kind of pride that the staff have about the image that they portray to the public.

Using your analytical and observational skills, you will be able to find crucial information about the company and its target audience. This kind of observation would help you much more than perusing the company website. If you keenly observe the ambience of a retail outlet or office you will be able to accumulate little tit-bits of information about its target audience as well as its employee relation policies.

The ambience of the office can also tell you whether the organization is a stickler for discipline and likes its employees to be dressed impeccably or whether they have a more casual approach towards work. These things might seem quite trivial initially, but they might have a long lasting impact during your interview. For example many Advertising agencies have quite a casual and open work culture. If you appraise the office ambience prior to your interview you won't turn up there for your interview in a three piece suit.

7. Six Degrees of Separation: Networking for prospective Job Interviews

Researchers of Columbia University have been toiling to establish this "six degrees" theory that everyone is somehow connected to everyone else. They claim that this theory is applicable for job hunters too. Even if you put this theory to test, you will be surprised with the results. Recent research work shows that, if you apply your networking skills properly you might only be six degrees away from making contact with your coveted job resource.

Often it happens that you desperately want a job but you cannot find a way to be in direct communication with the hiring manager, who is the only person to decide whether you are the right candidate for the job. Initially, this might seem like an uphill task, but if you apply proper interpersonal skills, you might be closer to contacting that hiring manager than you think.

You would be surprised to find that it is a small world when it comes to working. Your family or friends might refer you to someone they know who works in a reputed company. This might get you the greatest break in your life. Some times it becomes much easier to get a job if you know someone working in the same place where you want to work.

However, accepting help from former colleagues or business contacts in this regard is often more fruitful than taking the help of family friends. To make direct contact with your prospective employers, first you have to identify your dream job. For example, if you think that your ideal position would be working as a Senior Business Consultant, then zero on that post. Then it's only a matter of tapping the professional wells dug throughout your career years. Instead of just the regularly hyped advice to network with peers and friends, the focus needs to be much more directed toward professional contacts.

Try to shoot business like e-mails to make it clear to them that you are trying to find out about those esteemed employers who are hiring Senior Business Consultants. When you have got the name of those companies hiring Senior Business Consultants, your next step would be to zero on the best prospective employer and try to find out about their Hiring Manager.

Try to include every personal and professional tidbit you can scour in research—the hiring manager's alma mater, his personal interests, almost everything. This might seem trivial at first but your never know which tit-bit of information might open a connection with him and which in turn might secure an interview for you.

If getting hold of the name of the Hiring manager from your contacts is beyond your limit, try to at least find out about a person who holds a senior position in the organization and you can take your contacts further from there.

Moving on…..

Now as you have picked up an application form and would like to apply for a position, you need to consider a few other things as well. Before you fill up the application form, ask yourself – 'Do I have a proper resume to hand in with my application?' Having a resume indicates to the employer that you are a professional, detail oriented person. It shows that you are able to communicate verbally, express yourself and your accomplishments.

In this chapter we will focus on filling the application form properly, and in the next chapter will focus on resume writing.

Filling up the Application Form

Filling up the application form correctly and properly plays an important part in determining whether you get an opportunity of a job interview or not. Employers place a great importance when it comes to hiring, on how the application is being filled. This is the initial step to sort qualified applicants from non qualified ones.

Why is that?

Huge numbers of people fail to land good jobs simply because they don't fill in the application form in a correct manner. You can maximize your chances of being picked for an interview by using these following hints and tips. In many cases the employers judge on the basis of the following criteria.

1. Is your hand writing neat or messy?

Many employers judge their prospective job applicants on the basis of their handwriting too. Many applications get filled without care and in many cases are not legible enough. If your hand writing is neat it reflects that you are neat and you care about presentation. On the other hand, a shabbily filled out job application form which is pretty illegible, might stamp you as a careless and ignorant person.

Even if you have a scrawny handwriting, while filling your job application form try to put in an effort to make it as neat as possible. You should remember there are job applicants galore, and no body would take the trouble to peruse your application form with its untidy and illegible handwriting. It would simply be dumped in a dustbin.

2. Is the form filled in correctly and neatly?

It is important that you take the time and fill the application correctly. A large number of applications contain too many spelling errors, words crossed over and re-written in inappropriate places.

Try to avoid this sort of error because that would surely create a negative impression about you in the minds of your prospective employers. A grammatically error-free and correctly filled in application form bears testimony to your comprehension skills as well as literary skills. In the course of your job, you might need to fill out various important forms for your employers and if you are unable to fill up your application form correctly, no body is going to consider you seriously as a deserving candidate.

3. Does the form match what the resume shows?

Make sure the information that you provided on the application, matches what you have written on the resume. It is important to maintain consistency in both.

If the information provided in the application form doesn't match your resume then that might cast aspirations on your integrity and ethics. Whatever information you provide in your resume, like -the total years of work experience you have, or the grades that you received in College, must be identical to what you write out in your application form. If while filling out your application forms you cannot remember certain details pertaining to your work experience or academic qualifications, you should always double check rather than making a guess.

4. Did you take the time to fill the form completely?

Don't leave any portion of the application form blank. If you don't know the details, bring the application home with you. Find out the necessary details, fill up the complete form and then only submit the application form.

If you fill up the application partially and write in the required spaces "see resume", this might indicate you are not detail oriented and that you cut corners. As the adage goes there is no short cut to success and this time tested adage is also applicable while filling out the application forms too. A neatly filled out application form which contains all the relevant details would surely underscore the effort and time you have devoted to it. This in turn would highlight your qualities of meticulousness and diligence.

5. What are the gaps in your history?

If there are gaps in your educational history or work experience, you should not try to white- wash these gaps while filling out your application form. You should openly acknowledge these gaps, exactly the way you have done in your resume.

You might feel that if you avoid mentioning these gaps in your work experience and educational background, it might at least help you to get an interview. However, this kind of thinking is totally erroneous. Most employers tally the details in the application forms with those provided in the résumé, and if any instance of prevarication takes place you would be accused of duplicity of facts. As a result, your long cherished dream of joining that organization would be dashed to the grounds.

6. What is your availability?

Many employers look for employees who are flexible regarding working in different shifts which include evenings and week ends. This is particularly true when it comes to retail establishments. Restricting your availability might not get you an interview.

However, if you are a student trying to land a part time job, then you should fill out your available hours in detail so that there is no confusion regarding this later if you are chosen for the job.

7. What are your salary expectations?

Do not put any wage or salary expectation in your application which is unrealistic or out of the market range. Many people place themselves out of the market by requesting an unrealistic wage. At the same time you shouldn't let yourself be fleeced by asking a salary which is far less than the current market rate.

You should always try to find out what the going market range is and write the range. If this is your first job and you are unsure of what should be your expected salary, you can either search the internet for some hints about the current market rate, or else you can even ask some of your friends or relatives who are working in similar positions. In most cases the expected salary a person quotes gets determined by what he was earning in his last job.

However, in certain cases you might make an exception to this rule too. This is especially true in those cases when you might consider a change in your field of work. What ever salary you might have drawn as an experienced personnel in your previous job might not be offered if you are joining as a junior executive, without any relevant experience, in another field of work.

If you were making higher wages in your previous job and you are applying for a place which does not offer the same wages you might not state your wages on the application or make it clear that you are not looking for the same wages.

8. What position are you applying for?

Do not put "for anything" in those rows of your application form which require you to state the position you are applying for. This is a cardinal mistake which many job hunters commit. If you commit such a mistake it would only emphasize the fact that you don't bother about your career and you don't know where you fit in. It would also highlight the fact that you are not concerned enough and you have not done your homework about the company as well as the job.

Before you start filling out the application form you should always try to find out the job vacancies available and then prioritize as per your own skill set. However, in certain cases you might apply for more than one position. But, in such cases you should make sure that you clearly mention names of the positions you are applying for.

9. Do you have any criminal records?

You should be mentally prepared that your employers would do a background check for criminal records and for credit history. If you have filed for bankruptcy in the past or if you have served a jail term, be prepared that your prospective employers might dig out such skeletons out of the cupboard.

The back ground checks done by employers also could include information about your social networking accounts too. So, if you are job hunting try to avoid such web positing on your social networking accounts like Face book or Twitter which might act against you. In current times, employers are quite net savvy too. They even take into consideration the web postings or micro blogs posted by the job applicants in different social networking websites.

Most employers have an equal opportunity policy and if during your back ground check they find any postings which might not be in good taste or which might not be politically correct, or racially biased it might seriously hinder your job prospects.

10. What are your job goals and personal interests?

Most application forms have certain sections which require you to state your job goals or to elucidate why you have chosen to apply for this particular job. It is that part of the application form where you get to harp on your strengths and explain why you want the job. In this section you should elaborately dwell on your reasons for wanting this particular job, and what positive facets you can bring to the role. This section of an application form is equivalent to a ***covering letter***. So it must hold immense importance and should be filled up with utmost care.

If you are asked about your hobbies or out of work interest you should make sure you sound like an interesting person. Simply listing computer games, clubbing and surfing the net as hobbies, might make you seem too much of a frivolous and superficial person. So, be sure to add some creative hobbies while mentioning your hobbies and interests in your application form.

11. What are your ideas about Racial Equality?

Many application forms these days may also be an equality monitoring section, either as part of the form or as a separate piece of paper. This section usually contains an array of question about your racial tolerance and your adherence to the tenets of equal opportunity. It is always better to avoid any statements which might be interpreted as politically incorrect or racially biased. Making such statements which reek of racial bias might prove to be a serious deterrent in the course of your job hunt.

How to fill applications properly:

1. Have two copies of the application form so that if you make mistakes on one you have a spare one to fill correctly.

2. Read and re-read the form completely and carefully before you fill it; and if possible fill the information on a separate

piece of paper first. Once you are convinced that it is correct and complete then transfer the information to the application form.

3. When you have finished filling the application form, make sure you read it over and over again. Check for errors in spelling, incorrect dates, starting and ending dates of your previous jobs, school stating and ending dates, diplomas, certificates or degrees obtained. Also make sure the information matches the information on your resume.

4. Place in a folder to avoid any damage and to protect it from spillage. This sounds basic but is really very important. Have you seen application forms with dog ears or coffee spills? What did you think? I certainly have turned many applications down due to the above reasons.

CHAPTER 3

WHERE TO BEGIN

"We judge ourselves by what we feel capable of doing, but others judge us by what we have already done." ~ Henry Longfellow

The first step which you need to focus upon while looking for job is to have a proper resume.

What is a Resume?

A resume is also known as a Curriculum Vitae (CV). It is a snap-shot summary of your life till the present date. A resume usually contains factual summary of your education, work related experiences and professional growth.

What is the purpose of a Resume?

The real purpose of the resume is to sell your self in the human resource market. The objective is to present your self to unseen potential employers with the purpose of obtaining an opportunity of getting interviewed while seeking employment.

What should be the length of a Resume?

Depending on your experience, your resume should not be more than one or two pages. If your objective is clear, two pages are more than enough for an excellent resume. You don't want to make it too long or too complicated to follow, when it is reviewed by a potential employer. The employers are pressed for time and each job posting may attract hundreds of applicants. The person in charge of screening resumes does not have much time in his hand. Therefore, your resume, if not written well, or is too cluttered or wordy, might not make it to the top of the pile.

When you are preparing your resume, remember, your hobby does not get you a job. They are unimportant; so if you are running out of space just ignore them. Avoid putting controversial information in your resume, which might work against you like your religion, your church affiliation or being a part of groups that invoke controversy. Keep it simple, to the point and focus on your experience and accomplishments.

Before I move ahead to a brief discussion on the styles of resume writing, which are most popular, let me ask you a simple question. How would you personally define the word 'RESUME' if you were asked to denote what each alphabet of this particular word stood for?

Difficult? Not really, if you mentally consider the implications that this word, 'resume', generates.

For instance, after a little deliberation, I would like to expand the word **RESUME** to something like a **'Record of Employment Suitability and Useful Manipulation of Expertise'**. I genuinely feel that such an expansion of the word brilliantly encapsulates its basic purpose, which is precisely to fetch employment. Every employment or job has certain eligibility criteria, which may be termed as 'suitability' and which the employment seeker has to fulfill in order to obtain that particular job. To facilitate the whole process, a resume is prepared.

Ideally, a resume should clearly record, in a systematic manner, your skills, past experiences and accomplishments (if any) that are favorable to get hold of a specific job. This also entails a manipulative account of your expertise that is closely related to the job that you wish to apply for. In fact, you may be a proficient worker with adequate knowledge or know-how for a specific position or a particular job, but only when you appropriately record it in the form of a resume, can you think of securing it. Indeed, your most coveted job will always elude you until you have created your selling tool in the form of a resume, which is no more than a documentation of the qualities, attributes as well as performances that are most suitable to grab the job that you are looking for.

To delve deeper into the connotations of the word, *'resume'*, let us pause here and further analyze every word of the phrase, *'Record of Employment Suitability and Useful Manipulation of Expertise'*, a probable and highly relevant expansion of the root word.

To begin with, the first word of the phrase, namely, *'record'* is an extremely potential word as far as the implications of a resume are concerned. A record, to put it simply, is a document that offers valid information about "past events", and in the domain of employment, about past exposure and experiences. In other words, a record may be treated as a "permanent evidence" of your previous qualifications, skill-set and even accomplishments. The explanation of the word, 'record', itself gives a clear indication about its significance in the field of employment. Whenever you are seeking employment, your past record becomes critically important. This is precisely because your prospective employer would like to determine your qualifications and abilities through your record in order to find out whether you are suitable for that particular job or not.

In fact, a record is something which is indispensable in one's professional field or career. Say for example, if you are applying for the post of a teacher in a school, your employer would definitely wish to gain information about your academic background (specifically your scores or grades at different levels) and your past experience as a teacher (if any). To make it short, he would be interested in your academic record. Likewise, no matter whatever job you apply for, your past record of services will definitely be taken into account. In fact, the record, which takes the form of a resume, not only helps the employer in selecting the best candidate for a specific opening, but also helps those seeking jobs, to showcase their expertise and potentialities.

With that, let us move to the next word, 'employment' or the "state of being employed or having a job". As is quite obvious, the preparation of a resume is your first step towards seeking an employment. Just placed beside the word 'employment' is the word 'suitability', and it would be a nice thing to club them together and find out what sense the phrase makes. 'Suitability', as we all know, is suitableness for a "specific purpose", and here, for a specific job or position. Therefore, 'employment suitability' hints at the qualities, skills, experiences that are necessary for a particular post or profession. For instance, the employment suitability or employment criteria of a trading house could be knowledge of generating excise invoices and handling Excise Software with a minimum of 5 years of experience. Another concern looking for a PHP developer may frame its employment suitability as sound knowledge of Mysql, PHP, C, C++, Python, Perl, SEO, ecommerce, ability to offer solutions to complicated, multi-dimensional problems and a minimum of 3 years of related experience. In such a situation, your resume or record will testify as to whether you are most suitable for and meet the criteria of a particular service or not.

We now move to the next word in the phrase, which is *'useful'*, which, once again I would prefer to explain in conjunction with the following word *'manipulation'*. *'Manipulation'* means "the act or practice of manipulating" or controlling something skillfully, usually to serve a purpose. In the case of a resume, it would mean a careful handling and influencing of data so as to aptly meet the requirements of a job. An illustration of useful manipulation of information in a resume will do well to explain what I mean by it. Say, a person has Bachelors in Computer Science (B.E.) and Masters in Finance (MBA). If this person is applying to an IT based concern, he will emphasize on his IT skills and IT projects and just make a mention of his finance background as an added qualification. On the other hand, if he has been called for an interview by a financial company, he will manipulate his academic and professional data, so that his resume upholds his prowess in the financial domain more than in IT field.

This is exactly what *useful manipulation of expertise* means when we are talking of a resume. To drive in the point, let me give you another simple instance. A woman has Masters Degree in both English literatures as well as in Music. If this lady appears for an interview for the post of a music teacher, she will focus on her qualifications and achievements in the realm of music. But if she is to be interviewed for the position of an English teacher, her resume should highlight her qualifications and experience (if any) in the relevant field of literature.

Finally, we come to the last word, *'expertise'*. Expertise is usually defined as "skill or knowledge in a particular area". After all, each and every job or opening calls for a definite set of skills and know-how for one to be eligible for a particular job. And the candidates whose resumes reflect the most appropriate qualifications and expertise for a specific work are lucky enough to be short-listed and given a call for an interview by that concern.

Having said all that, I hope by this time you are completely aware of all the possible insinuations that the word 'resume' creates. You must also have been able to register the fact that your resume is your foremost move towards getting that much-awaited interview call.

So, now would you like to make an attempt to give another expansion of the word 'Resume', which, according to you, would be a crisp presentation of the meaning that the word holds for you? Now it's time to cast a glance at the most widespread formats or styles of writing a resume.

What are the common resume styles?

There are two main styles of resumes:

1. **Chronological Resume**: This is the most commonly used format/style that most of the employers are familiar with. This format lists records of events or employment in a chronological order beginning with most current achievement or employment first and continues until your last employment. The advantage of this format is that, it builds credibility and shows progress and growth over time. This is an excellent way to build your resume if you have a long career history which has shown progress over time. This style is not recommended for a person who is entering the job market for the first time.

2. **Functional Resume**: This enlists your experience or skills. It does not focus on where and when you obtained the skill or the experience; rather it places employment history into sections. This is best used when you are entering the market for the first time with limited or no experience, for example, if you are a high school student, university student, or a graduate. This is also good for home makers, older workers, and people with plenty of volunteer work experience and those with gaps in their work history. Some employers don't prefer this style. This is because; they cannot ascertain the dates of employment or gauge the reasons for gaps in employment.

The following templates will show how each format of resume should look like.

Template Chronological Resume

Full name

Street Address Town, State or Province Zip (Postal) Code

Phone Number _____

Objective: List your job objective here, be very specific and keep it within 6-10 words.

Work History

<Dates of Employment> <Place of Employment>

<Job Title> <City, State or Province>

- Job Responsibility/Specific Accomplishments and Promotions, if applicable.

- Job Responsibility/Specific Accomplishments.

- Job Responsibility/Specific Accomplishments.

<Dates of Employment> <Place of Employment>

<Job Title> <City, State or Province>

- Job Responsibility/Specific Accomplishments and Promotions, if applicable.

- Job Responsibility/Specific Accomplishments.

- Job Responsibility/Specific Accomplishments.

<Dates of Employment> <Place of Employment>

<Job Title> <City, State or Province>

- Job Responsibility/Specific Accomplishments and Promotions, if applicable.

- Job Responsibility/Specific Accomplishments.

Education

\<Dates Attended> \<School Name>

\<Area of Study or Degree> \<City, State or Province>

- Degree Minor school activities, clubs involved with, awards or scholarships, if applicable.

Other Experience

- List other related experience, skills or computer programs that are relevant to the job you are seeking.

References

- Available upon request.

Template Functional Resume

Full Name

Street Address Town State or Province Zip (Postal) Code

Phone Number _____

Objective: List your job objective here, be very specific and keep it short within 6-10 words.

☐ *Qualifications and Skills*

- Qualification or Skills related to the job you are seeking.

- Qualification or Skills related to the job you are seeking.

- Qualification or Skills related to the job you are seeking.

- Qualification or Skills related to the job you are seeking.

- Qualification or Skills related to the job you are seeking.

- Qualification or Skills related to the job you are seeking.

- Qualification or Skills related to the job you are seeking.

- Qualification or Skills related to the job you are seeking.

☐ *Work History*

- \<Dates > \<Job Title> \<Company> \<City, State or Province>

- \<Dates > \<Job Title> \<Company> \<City, State or Province>

- \<Dates > \<Job Title> \<Company> \<City, State or Province>

- \<Dates > \<Job Title> \<Company> \<City, State or Province>

Education

<Dates Attended> <School Name>

<Area of Study or Degree> <City, State or Province>

- Degree Minor school activities, clubs involved with, awards or scholarships, if applicable.

Other Experience

- List other related experience, skills or computer programs that are relevant to the job you are seeking. You can also list military service, community work, volunteer services, etc...

References

- Available upon request.

Sample Functional Resume

Mary Smith

123 Broadway Street
New market, Ontario L3Y 6X2

(905) 444-2651

Objective: Executive Assistant

Key Qualifications:

- Attention to detail - Strong organizational and computer skills.

- Strong interpersonal, customer service and time management skills.

- Over 10 years experience in a fast paced customer/client service environment.

- Independent in thought and action, with ability to follow direction and meet deadlines and goals

- Certification in administrative assistance.

Relevant Experience and Skills:

- Handled *all* administrative details on designated projects - set-up templates and performed follow-up with department administrators and managers to ensure deadlines.

- Monitored meeting of processes and objectives, and reporting to the President.

- Maintained processes and procedures to ensure consistent performance of routines and reporting.

- Interacted with internal departments and external clients on President's behalf, as requested, via face-to-face, email or phone

- Prepared purchase orders, expense reports, business plans and correspondence for President's signature.

- Scheduled internal and external meetings like, set-up and take-down meetings (book facilities, refreshments, lunch etc.)

- Prepared and circulated meeting agendas in advance.

- Recorded proceedings according to minutes of the meetings where necessary.

- Ensured that the President has all necessary files and documents for meetings at hand.

- Arranged travel and accommodations through internal or outside agents.

- Researched information as requested on various projects.

- Assured discreet handling of all business - treated information as confidential.

Employment:

United Insurance Brokers Toronto, Ont
Executive assistant May 2001 to Present

Upper Court House Toronto, Ontario
Secretary Dec. 1998 to April 2001

Education:

University of British Columbia British Columbia
B.A Administrative Assistant 1995 to 1998

References: Available upon request

Sample Chronological Resume

John Smith

86 Eagle Street
Toronto, Ontario M2K 6N5

(416) 456-7841

Objective: Retail sales Associate

Employment:

2006 To Present   Super Electronic Store
Sales Associate Electronics   **Toronto, ON.**

- Maintained a high level of product and service knowledge, customer service, professional appearance, demeanor, and attitude at all times.

- Participated in merchandising and promotional activities, ensuring transactional, inventorial and procedural accuracy.

- Worked in partnership with Store Managers and other employees to maximize store sales and in-store presence.

- Ability to make excellent sales to achieve performance aligned with company's goals and objectives, with excellent customer service, interpersonal, organizational and communication skills.

- Motivated and creative team player, with interest in management and career growth.

- Had won '*SALES Person of the month award* in retail sales'.

- Proficient in computer usage with basic programs such as Windows Office.

2005 To 2006   ABC Electronics
Product Sales   **Hamilton, ON**

- Supervised two sales associates.

- Maintained familiarity with all major product lines.

- Conducted weekly inventory.

- Monitored regularly the availability of stock.

- Ordered supplies for retail sales from all major suppliers.

- When I was given responsibility for ordering and selling Batteries, sales, gross margin increased by 20%.

Education:

Douglas College Hamilton, ON
Retail Sales 2005
Diploma in Sales and Customer Service

Cardinal High School Hamilton
Grade 12 Diploma 2002

References: Available upon request

Helpful Hints about Resume Writing

1. Focus on accomplishments, not Duties - Many job seekers fill their resume with what they do. Example filled orders, assist customers, filled legal forms, assist lawyers etc. These duty words do not sell you and it doesn't highlight your accomplishments. It does not get your resume on the top of short-listed candidates. Whatever your job is, be it permanent, temporary, part time or full time, you need to consider and analyze what you have gained from the experience and what was your contribution to it.Organizing your thought in this manner helps the employer get a better picture of your potential and it also helps to communicate clearly what you have to offer to your prospective employer. You must consider mentioning any achievement, rewards and recognition that you have received from your current or previous employer. Information concerning whether you have ever been the "Employee of the month", or you won any awards, you had ever got a day off with pay, etc. should all be mentioned in the company news letter.

2. Avoid uncomfortable Phrases – For every word that you write in your resume, you must be able to explain them comfortably. This is why, you should avoid putting down comments that you will find difficult to explain. Say, when someone writes on the resume "I am hard working", I ask them, "Tell me about your hard working, how you define hard work?" Almost in 90% of the cases, I receive an "Ugh…" Therefore, avoid being vague and mention only such skills and qualities, which one can measure on an objective basis. When you say that you played a key role in improving the efficiency of your previous company, you are being undeniably vague, but when you clearly note that you helped your company by cutting down the requisition costs by 20% in a particular fiscal year, it is bound to impress your prospective employer.

3. Write brief and straight sentences- You must note that a resume is a succinct record or document that gets about 30 seconds to be scanned. In that case, do not go for long-winding sentences and lengthy paragraphs but rather brief and straight statements to put forth your knowledge, skills and experiences. Make a note of the fact that the more concise and to-the-point your resume is, the better it has chances to grab the immediate attention of the employer.

4. Use action words – The best way to communicate your results and accomplishments is through use of action words. Using action verbs will make it very easy for you to paint the picture.

• Accelerated	• Programmed
• Augmented	• Improvised
• Achieved	• Incorporated
• Awarded	• Implemented
• Assisted	• Launched
• Accomplished	• Negotiated
• Budgeted	• Operated
• Conceptualized	• Participated
• Coached	• Won
• Convinced	• Solved
• Consolidated	• Increased
• Coordinated	• Trained
• Customized	• Honed
• Implemented	• Hired
• Negotiated	• Guided
• Communicated	• Generated
• Published	• Governed
• Oversaw	• Handled
• Developed	• Reduced
• Delegated	• Performed
• Devised	• Saved
• Decided	• Facilitated
• Demonstrated	• Fulfilled
• Established	• Finalized
• Executed	
• Energized	
• Estimated	
• Evaluated	
• Enforced	
• Recommended	

Believe it or not, such power-packed words will definitely be noticed by your prospective employer and will work miracles in getting your resume short-listed. It goes without saying that positive action words have an inherent power in them and will do well to uplift your resume by releasing affirmative vibes.

5. Handle personal data prudently– Even though it is best to treat your resume as a professional record, it is advisable that you present your personal data in a manner that suits the job as well as the company that you are applying to. This means that however much or little of your personal information might be reflected in your resume, it will determine what kind of job you are looking for and in which domain or concern. For instance, there are certain prospective employers who wish to gain an insight into the personal life of a prospective employee just to find out to what extent the person is serious and sincere about that particular employment, and thereby determine whether his recruitment would be long-term or not. At times, it is a person's diligence, which is mirrored through a personal situation in his previous employment that is gauged when considering him for his new post. For instance, an air-hostess had gone out of her way to save a passenger at a time of crisis is definitely not a professional data as far as the record of the lady is concerned. But a mention of it, perhaps as an achievement, is bound to grab the attention of the airlines to which she later applies. After all, every employer looks for an employee who will be beneficial to his organization on a long term basis, and no one wants to go on looking for new recruits at frequent intervals. Of course there are exceptions to this. Employers who have the tendency of exploiting the employees cannot hold back a good employee for a long term, and are bound to look for new recruits through recurrent interviews.

Here I must say that you as a prospective employee should know what and how much to say about your personal life to your prospective employer. Make sure that you neither reveal too much as it might put the employer in an advantageous position to exploit you at some level, nor too little of personal data, which would not allow the employer to gauge whether recruiting you would be valuable for his company or not. In other words, in your resume, be careful and wise in dealing with your personal data.

However, giant corporate houses do not bother much about personal data and strictly focus on professional records.

6. Include non job related experiences – It is important to include non job related experiences and achievements, especially, if you don't have much work experience. Try to make it as an added value, to the position which you are applying for. Focus on areas that gained you leadership skills, team work and communication skills. Say for example, if you have been a great elocutionist in your school and college days, it would be good to make a mention of it in your resume. Your prospective employer might wish to utilize your oratorical skills to his advantage and prefer you over some other candidate meeting the employment criteria. Again, it is always a great idea to pen down your experiences (if any) as a leader, as that would be a clear indication of your ability to take up responsibilities and handle people. And there is not even a single organization, which will not value such above average qualities.

7. Make your Resume fool proof- It is imperative that you proofread your resume times and again before taking out a printable version. A typo in your resume predicts that you are far from the job that you have applied for. So do pay serious attention to every minute detail in your resume and make sure that it is absolutely devoid of spelling mistakes or grammatical errors.

8. Make your resume easy for the eyes- See to it that the visual appeal of your resume is comfortable and easy for the eyes. To ensure that make use of standard margins, which means leave 1 inch space on the top and the bottom and 1.25 inches space for the two sides. It is essential that your resume does not have a crammed and claustrophobic look. So it is recommended that you leave adequate breathing space between one section and the next. As already mentioned, make use of tables and bulleted patterns in your resume, as and when it is necessary. Coming to the font styles, it is better to bank on simple yet formal fonts rather than the exotic, curved or unusual ones.

9. Use colored paper for your resume- When you have finished structuring your resume, make copies in different color papers like light grey or beige. Almost 99% of the resumes received are in white color paper. Selecting different colors almost guarantees the fact that it will be looked at. It increases employer curiosity. But make sure that you go for such colored papers which are sober and possess a corporate feel. After all, your resume should act as your window to the professional world, and thus it is very important that it has the right kind of look. Here I would like to add that it would be better for you to select the color of the resume paper on the basis of a few considerations like the type of concern, its magnitude, the kind of job you are applying for as well as any possible preference of the employer (if you have a prior idea about it).

It is your resume, which will help the employer create an impression about you even when he has not met you. Under such circumstances, if your resume is typed on a colored paper, the employer will, first, like the change, and second, will think that you are in some way different from the other candidates who have applied for that same post as you have taken an initiative to be different. But I repeat that you can be experimental with the color of the paper on which you print your resume only after considering its consequences. This is due to the fact that some concerns and companies are extremely rigid in their approach and may not appreciate your endeavor of using a colored paper for your resume.

10. Keep your papers together- Ensure that your resume and application forms are stapled together to avoid it getting separated and lost amongst pile of resumes. You can place it in a duo-tang.

Now that you are more or less aware of the ways and means to prepare an appropriate resume, its time to move ahead to the next important aspect, which is the cover letter. Your cover letter, if it is attached to your resume, which it should ideally be, is the first document the interview screener will be reading about you. It is true that most prospective employees, when applying for different positions, do not bother much about cover letters. I, personally, receive many resumes with no cover letters attached to them. But, it goes without saying that a resume with a cover letter scores much above one without it. In fact, resumes with impressive cover letters are the ones, which find a place on the top of the short list pile.

In my opinion, people who take the time to write cover letters are, generally speaking, confident communicators with an added flair in writing. Most important, they are people, who, according to me, have the ability to think logically, precisely because a cover letter is nothing but a logical and fierce argument to sell your self to the employer. Moreover, a cover letter is an apt tool to create a good impression in the mind of the person who will be interviewing you, and consequently, it should compel them to take a look at your resume and give you a chance for an interview.

What are cover letters?

Cover letters are also known as motivational letters or job application letters. It is an introductory letter that comes as an attachment to a resume or curriculum vitae.

Basically, cover letters are expected to provide some additional set of information on your skills and experience besides those which have been mentioned in your resume. They explain why you should be apprehended as the most suitable and qualified candidate for the respective job applied for. To put it simply, cover letters should focus on your specific skills and experiences that are mostly relevant to the requirements of the job in question. What is more, cover letters should be carefully tailored towards what you want your prospective employer to know about you in not more than three or four paragraphs. Therefore, preparing a proper cover letter is the first and the most important aspect of the application process that you need to perform while seeking employment.

In a professional set up, if your resume is not accompanied by an appropriate cover letter, it will be like walking in for an interview without even shaking hands. A cover letter basically acts as a mirror image of the respective individual. A properly designed and formatted cover letter can spark off the interest of your employer and help you to create an impression that spells competence. It is thus mandatory that the pitch or tone of your cover letter should be powerful, organized and a reflection of your personality and potentials.

In other words, a cover letter provides you with the opportunity of putting across your principal focus and dedicated energy towards the job aspired for. Human resource experts point out that an effective cover letter can be advantageous to a particular candidate who does not possess the required experience called for a particular job.

In addition, an effective cover letter should provide a perfect explanation as to why you are interested in a specific company or organization. Your cover letter should talk about something special that you like about that company. Say for instance, you may write that "I am very delighted to know that your company finds a place in the top 50 best employers in the country", and then go ahead and add that "It shows you value your employees and your employees value you." By appreciating the company's commitment to work-life balance in your cover letter, you have already impressed your interviewer.

Why should you have a cover letter?

You should prepare your cover letter with certain objectives in mind. As already mentioned, the foremost objective should be to provide important additional details about yourself along with the relevance of your candidature to the job you have applied for. The intent is to convince your future employer and kindle his interest in your resume. He or she should eventually resolve to call you for an interview.

There are different aspects to it:

- You need to present your self as a quick learner. Project your self as an honest and a hard-working individual. Make optimum usage of the precious space in your cover letter. Say something that is interesting, exciting and equally relevant.

- Through a cover letter, you need to present the appropriate premises that can direct towards the desired conclusion. You need to state that the skills that you have cultivated through learning and experience can effectively cater to the present requirements of the company. Use the cover letter to show that the qualifications, skills and achievements that you have attained are directly connected with those which the employer is seeking.

- A positive and optimistic attitude is a pre-requisite when you desire success. Each individual in the professional world is himself a brand and this entails that he/she has his own Unique Selling Point. An applicant can use the cover letter to effectively present and use his USP in the job market.

- Through a cover letter an applicant can easily describe how his previous job has provided him with the necessary experience and helped him to attain the skills that are required for the job. The objective should be to explain how you can contribute to the progress of the company.

A good and thorough research on the company and the respective industry that it is a part of is important prior to submitting your application. The knowledge that you have gained on this account can be effectively displayed through your cover letter. In fact, it will make your cover letter more convincing and impressive as it will be a demonstration of your enthusiasm and earnestness.

What is the function of a cover letter?

The cover letter basically functions as a medium of communication between the applicant and the prospective employer. It works towards the creation of the first impression, and thus goes a long way in determining the position that an applicant can expect to attain in the respective company and the industry as a whole.

- A Cover letter is an explanation on why you are sending your resume. It is a specific documentation on what you are basically seeking, your objective. It clarifies before your prospective employer whether you are looking for an opportunity for internship during the summers, or you are on a look out for a permanent position after the completion of your graduation. You may also express your desire to know more on the future employment possibilities in the sector.

- Your prospective employer is always interested to know on how you have come to know about the company and its requirements. Through a cover letter, an applicant can specifically mention the manner in which he got acquainted with the position and the organization. If it is on recommendation or suggestion of a person that you have applied for a particular job to a company, you must make a mention of his/her name, preferably at the beginning of your cover letter.

- To repeat, since, it is the cover letter that your employer will come across in the first place it should be highly persuasive in approach. The function of a cover letter gets effectively fulfilled when it adequately targets the employer in a well-written and focused manner.

- A cover letter is expected to present some additional information than what is already mentioned in your resume. This entails that you can use the cover letter to focus on the important and interesting elements that are there in your background. They can be alternative educational qualifications and degrees or may be your experiences in leadership.

- A cover letter being the initial mode of communication should be projected as a perfect reflection of your attitude. Present it as a mirror to your qualities. The essential attributes that count a lot in the professional world, irrespective of the diverse fields, should also find a place in your cover letter. To name a few of them would be- enthusiasm, dedication, diligence, motivation and effective communication skills.

What should you include in your cover letter?

A cover letter must look like a typical business letter, and so its basic format should be akin to it. There are three broad aspects that a cover letter needs to cater to:

1. The first paragraph of your cover letter should indicate the purpose of your writing it.

2. In the middle paragraphs you should specify the details that you wish to offer to your prospective employer.

3. In the concluding paragraph, you should mention the manner in which you would like to follow up your letter.

When it comes to writing a cover letter, it must always have the name of a contact person. Even if the advertisement or web posting does not indicate the name, make an endeavor to find out the company's phone number or the recruiting agency's phone number. Call them, and you may have to speak to a secretary, a human resource person or if it is a local store branch, to the store manager. When you call up, make sure that you mention that you are applying for the position posted in the newspaper and would like to know the name of the person to whom the application should be directed to.

A cover letter covers three common categories of purpose. As you mention on why you are writing the cover letter, make sure that you point out your reference. Your reference might be a friend, acquaintance or a relative. As already mentioned, if he or she is a mutual contact of you and your prospective employer, the mentioning of the name is likely to enhance the interest of the reader.

As mentioned in the beginning of the paragraph, your cover letter might be in:

1. Response to a job posting

2. You may be writing a prospecting letter

3. It may also be a networking letter

If you are responding to a job posting, there should be a clear indication regarding where you have learned about the position. The earnestness should be expressed through your enthusiasm. There ought to be a proper linkage between the credentials that you have mentioned and the qualifications required for the said position.

If your cover letter is a prospecting letter, the manner in which you enquire about the possible job openings is very important. The specific job objectives should be clearly stated. You should remember that this type of cover letter is unsolicited. Therefore, it becomes even more vital to catch the interest of the reader.

While you are writing a prospecting letter, your potential to cater to the requirements of the employer should be appropriately focused upon. It must never be the case that you simply end up asking on what the employer has got to offer you. The most common and effective way to address this issue is by providing evidence that you have done sufficient research on the respective organization and you have the crucial skills that the employer is seeking for. In a corporate environment, problem solving skills are always desirable. So, if you possess any achievements on this aspect, make sure to properly highlight them. This is an effective method to provide a sort of assurance to your prospective employer that they would make a great choice in selecting you. If you are writing a networking letter, it is understood that you are seeking information from some individual. In such circumstances, make it a point to be specific in your request.

As you reach the second part of your cover letter, you are expected to mention on what you have got to offer. This means that in this section, you must highlight your skills, strengths, accomplishments as well as the reasons why you consider yourself to be the most suitable candidate for that particular job. Here it is better to use the bullet format as that is bound to attract the attention of the reader. There should also be a proper illustration of the point that the specific abilities and the experience factor that is mentioned in the advertisement lies in perfect alignment with your achievements.

The final phase of your cover letter is the manner in which you are planning to follow up. This is the concluding part of your cover letter and, therefore, in this part you should reiterate your interest in the said position. Make your employer aware of the possibilities by which they can successfully reach you. Provide your telephone numbers along with your e-mail address. Finally close your letter with a humble request for a one-to-one meeting with the person concerned. And now your application process complete.

According to the popular format, a cover letter is not usually longer than one page, though exceptions are allowed with respect to the content. It is technically divided into a Header, Introduction, Body and Closing.

Header – Here the applicant's address and other related information is provided. The recipient or the prospective employer's contact information along with the date of application is also written.

Introduction –This section should state the particular position that you are applying for in a precise manner. The objective is to withhold the prospective employer's attention.

Body – The purpose of this section is to highlight or amplify the various aspects of your resume or job application. It must appear as an appropriate explanation on why the applicant is interested in the said position. It must also explain why he can prove to be a valuable resource to the employer. You can briefly discuss your specific skills, educational qualifications and past experiences, if any, with regard to the respective post.

Closing –This concluding section is a summation of the entire letter. It is an indication towards the following step that the applicant desires to take. It can either be a direct approach where he would make a call to follow up or it can be an indirect one. Finally comes the valediction section where you write 'sincerely' and then put your signature line. There can also be an abbreviation 'ENCL', which indicates that you have placed in some enclosures.

Bear in mind that making a good impression is the principle objective of a good cover letter. The structure and wording thus becomes extremely important. It is not customary to use more than four paragraphs in your cover letter. With respect to wording, there are few points to keep in mind:

- The expression should be professional but warm and friendly.

- The letter should be interesting to the reader. It should be informative and precise.

- Enthusiasm combined with selective assertion can be effective, provided, it does not appear pushy. On the other extremity, do not end up begging for a position!

- Natural and simple language is always welcome. Avoid clichés and certain expressions like 'aforementioned'.

- The words and the phrases that you use should spell positivism. Sentences that begin with, 'I have' or 'I can' always gives a good impression.

- Your selling points can be presented in a bullet format. Alternatively, you can make it more interesting by presenting them in a Comparison List Style. This means that you compare your respective experiences or professional qualifications and accomplishments with that of the requirements stated by the company.

• No expression that ends up weakening your message should be used. Phrases like 'fairly experienced' or 'some knowledge' are apprehended as lack of confidence.

• Remember, over assertion stinks of snobbishness. So, take note of it that you do not start every sentence or paragraph with 'I'.

Important Basic Points:

1. Use a clean, white, letter size paper.

2. Go for the basic font styles like Arial or Times New Roman.

3. Leave a decent amount of space surrounding the edges of the page.

4. There should also be enough space between each section and paragraph.

5. The overall appearance of the letter must be neat.

6. Strictly avoid photocopies or marked cover letters.

7. Writing a rough draft is always beneficial. It will provide coherence to your thoughts.

8. Remember, your cover letter is an example of your writing skills. Therefore, ensure that it is devoid of spelling and grammatical errors.

9. You must keep a copy of all the cover letters that you are sending. Apart from being used as a future reference, it will also help you remember the content and your argument during the interview.

GUIDELINES FOR A COVER LETTER

Your Street Address
City, State Zip Code
Telephone Number
Email Address

Month, Day, Year

Mr./Ms./Dr. First Name Last Name
Title
Name of Organization
Street or P. O. Box Address
City, State Zip Code

Dear Mr./Ms./Dr. Last Name:

Opening paragraph: State why you are writing; how you learned of the organization or position, and basic information about yourself.

2nd paragraph: Tell why you are interested in the employer or type of work the employer does (Simply stating that you are interested does not tell why, and can sound like a formal letter). Demonstrate that you know enough about the employer or position to relate your background to the employer or position. Mention specific qualifications which make you a good fit for the employer's needs. This is an opportunity to explain in more detail relevant items in your resume. Refer to the fact that your resume is enclosed. Mention other enclosures if such are required to apply for a position.

3rd paragraph: Indicate that you would like the opportunity to be interviewed for a position or to talk with the employer, to learn more about their opportunities or hiring plans. State what you will do to follow up, such as telephone the employer within two weeks. If you are scheduled to be in the employer's location and could offer to schedule a visit, indicate when. State that you would be glad to provide the employer with any additional information needed. Thank the employer for her/his consideration.

Sincerely,

(Your handwritten signature)

Your name typed

Enclosure(s) (refers to resume, etc.)

A Sample Cover Letter for the post
of a Senior Product Buyer

Amy Frost
249 Elizabeth Street,
New York City, NY 10014.
Cell Phone: 555-456-2121
Email: amy@adsol.com

April 29, 2009

Jonathan Parker
Meridian Systems
185 West, 27th Street
New York City, NY 10054.

Dear Mr. Parker,

It was in today's The New York Times that I came across an opening in your company for the position of a Senior Product Buyer and thought of making a strong case for myself. At present I am the Senior Product Buyer of Adriatic Solutions with more than six years of experience in computer hardware purchasing. It is my firm belief that I fulfill all your requirements and would make an ideal candidate for this post.

Listed below are some of the functions that I have successfully performed in the role of a Senior Product Buyer:

- Prepared specification of products and determined service requirements.

- Conducted extensive research on products and their utility.

- Played a pivotal role in obtaining proposal prices and delivery quotes.

- Have been responsible for timely delivery of products to customers.

- Improved gross margin by 3% through negotiation of a better deal with suppliers.

- Increased sales of accessories by 20% by introducing a new displayer to the stores.

Expertise in my work can be partly traced back to my Bachelor's degree in Business Administration along with a sound background in direct purchasing.

My dedication towards work have been recognized and commended all through my career by my previous employers. I strongly feel that I can live up to the expectations of a Senior Product Buyer of your company and prove the association to be a productive one.

It is a sheer privilege to become a part of a company that ranks in the list of Top 50 Employers. This clearly shows that you value your employees and your employees value you, and it also indicates that you are committed towards striking the perfect work-life balance.

I will look forward for a one-to-one meeting with you to discuss my qualification. You may contact me anytime via my cell phone (555-456-2121) or via email (amy@adsol.com)

Thank you for your time and consideration.

Sincerely,

Amy Frost

SAMPLE LETTER OF APPLICATION

123 Apartment Heights Dr.
Vancouver, BC
(604) 555-0101
abcd@cd.org

February 22, 2009

Dr. Michael Jr. Rhodes
Principal, Heritage Elementary School
1711 Blue Road
Bradford, Ontario

Dear Dr. Rhodes,

I enjoyed our conversation on February 18th at the Family and Child Development seminar on teaching young children and appreciated your personal input about helping children attend school for the first time. This letter is to follow-up about the Fourth Grade Teacher position as discussed at the seminar. I will be completing my Bachelor of Science Degree in Family and Child Development with a concentration in Early Childhood Education at Colombia College in May of 2009, and will be available for employment at that time.

The teacher preparation program at Colombia College includes a full academic year of student teaching. Last semester I taught second grade and this semester, fourth grade. These valuable experiences have afforded me the opportunity to:

- develop lesson plans on a wide range of topics and varying levels of academic ability,

- work with emotionally and physically challenged students in a total inclusion program,

- observe and participate in effective classroom management approaches,

- assist with parent-teacher conferences, and

- Complete In-Service sessions on diversity, math and reading skills, and community relations.

Through my early childhood education courses I have had the opportunity to work in a private day care facility, Rainbow Riders Childcare Center, and in Colombia College Child Development Laboratory. Both these facilities are Minstery accredited and adhere to the highest standards. At both locations, my responsibilities included leading small and large group activities, helping with lunches and snacks, and implementing appropriate activities. Both experiences provided me with extensive exposure to the implementation of developmentally appropriate activities and materials.

I look forward to putting my knowledge and experience into practice in the public school system. Next week I will be in Bradford, and I plan to call you then to answer any questions that you may have. I can be reached before then at (604) 555-7670. Thank you for your consideration.

Sincerely,

(handwritten signature)

Donna Harrington

Enclosure

SAMPLE LETTER OF APPLICATION

April 14, 2009

Mr. Rob Anderson
Employment Manager
ABC Company
789 Queen Street
Toronto, Ontario

M2Y 2X6
randerson@abc.com

Dear Mr. Anderson,

From your company's web site I learned about your need for a sales representative for the Toronto, North areas. I am very interested in this position with ABC Company, and believe that my education and employment background are appropriate for the position.

While working toward my master's degree, I was employed as a sales representative with a small dairy foods firm. I increased my sales volume and profit margin appreciably while at Farmer's Foods, and I would like to repeat that success in the Health industry. I have a strong academic background in biology and marketing, and think that I could apply my combination of knowledge and experience to the health industry. I will complete my master's degree in marketing in mid-May and will be available to begin employment in early June.

Enclosed is a copy of my resume, which more fully details my qualifications for the position.

I look forward to talking with you regarding sales opportunities with ABC Company. Within the next week I will contact you to confirm that you received my email and resume and to answer any questions you may have.

Ramzi Karim

Thank you for your consideration.

Sincerely,

David Jones
5542 Hunt Club
Ottawa, O3X 1B5
(613) 555-8082
djones@vt.edu

Resume attached as MS Word document (assuming company web site instructed applicants to do this)

CHAPTER 4

INTERVIEW FORMATS

"The gem cannot be polished without friction, nor man perfected without trials." ~ Chinese proverb

Before we go into the details of different interview formats, it is important to understand who the interviewers are, what they expect from you and what you should expect from them.

Interviewers come in different shapes and form depending on experience. The more junior the interviewer, the less experience they are.

Interviewers are public relation officers from human resource department or at times from operations department and in case of small companies they could be owners and operators. If they are trained well they are expert at judging others. They try to do their best to match people with jobs. Interviewers through rigorous and pre-prepared questions try to find out information to assess suitability for a position.

The job of an interviewer is not an easy one. They have a limited time to interview an individual, inorder to find out the truth as much as possible about a candidate by putting their own biases and stereotype a side.

How can you tell you are dealing with an experienced interviewer?

- They do not talk much rather they make you do the talking.

- They challenge you.

- They will put you on the spot.

- They scrutinize you.

- They expect you to defend what is on your resume.

- They respect the time spent with you by not allowing distractions during the interview.

- They answer your questions with truth.

There are many interview formats, which an applicant can go through on their search for employment. In this book we will be focusing on six different formats. They are-

1. **Individual :** One on one interviews

2. **Group interviews:** In this format multiple candidates are interviewed by one or more than one interviewer.

3. **Panel Interview:** One candidate with more than one interviewer.

4. **Campus interviews**

5. **Behavioral Interviews**

6. **Competency based interviews**

1. Individual interviews

Once you start getting the calls for interviews, the fun begins. Your journey towards landing a job with your favorite organization starts with a bang. Many organizations conduct more than one interview. In many cases you might have to face three interviews, before you can find out if you have a job or not. To be successful in an interview, you must be prepared for it. We are going to talk about preparation for the first interview, and then go into the detailed entailments of each interview and prepare you for each one of them.

Preparations:
First interview:

You have been waiting for this day for many months or perhaps many years. Finally, the moment of truth has arrived and you are to appear in your first ever interview for a job! The job may change the way you lead your life, and so, it is undoubtedly a golden opportunity for you. But you may miss this opportunity, if you are not prepared seriously and meticulously for this red letter day in your life. The further processes and finally securing the job depends upon this interview.

Some of the key points to know about first interviews are as follows:

- They are mostly conducted by junior recruiter or entry level manager or supervisors. Some are well trained and some not.

- They will be making the decision whether you go forward or not. So you need to impress them.

- They are very meticulous at digging information out of you. They are very cautious because they do not want to look bad in front of their supervisors by putting too many unsuitable candidates forward.

- They are very impressionable therefore it is important that you go to the interview well prepared.

It is needless to say that you will be very nervous. But if you follow certain basic rules, you will surely sail through the first round with flying colors. Here are a few of those very important tips.

- Dress up properly for the interview. You must have heard the adage "The first impression is the lasting impression"- so, you need to appear smartly dressed up.

- Hide your nervousness with a courteous smile. It will make the environment a bit lighter and you will feel a lot more confident.

- Have a positive body language, as that is the first thing that an interviewer will look for.

- Try to gain some basic information about the company in which you are appearing for the interview.

- Prepare answers to basic questions related to your hobbies, your ambitions, yourself, and your likes and dislikes. These questions come in handy in any interview.

Second Interview:

There is nothing, more exciting than, getting the call for a second interview. It means you passed the screening and that you are among the short list of people to be considered for a position with the company. Some companies hire between 2-10% of the candidates they interview. Therefore if the company hires 10% of the people they interview, it means that out of 100 interviews, if only 10 people made it through, you are one of the ten lucky ones. This means you will be competing with top ten candidates in the next round. It is important that you don't get over excited and feel that it is in the bag that you'll land the job. Second interviews are much more difficult than the first interviews and you will probably have to answer some tough and challenging questions.

Second interviews are normally conducted by more senior human resource managers, middle management and senior supervisors which mean they are well trained and more difficult to fool them.

You need to make sure that you follow the same steps you did when you got the first call over the phone. The person who is calling you for a second interview is probably the same person who conducted the first interview. Thank the person for putting you forward and ask them a few quick questions about your performance in the first interview.

Make sure you get the name of the person conducting the second interview, their position in the company, the time and the date right.

The person who is conducting the second interview is either the decision maker or will be passing you on for the third interview.

Third Interview:

Fantastic, you made it through the second interview and got the call for the third one!

Third interviews are normally conducted by final decision makers. The person who is conducting the interview may not be a Human Resource individual. Rather they are general managers, divisional sales managers, sales managers, operation managers or district managers of the company.

Third interviews at times are just a formality to get to meet the person who you probably will be working for or the person who makes the final decision on the hiring.

Third interviews are normally more relaxed and at times it will not necessarily focus on your resume or job experience but rather on intangible qualities like your communication skills, leadership skills, your attitude and interpersonal skills.

Third interviewers will normally evaluate how you fit in the organization and will also look for anything else that they might have missed in the past two interviews. They also try to verify what was discussed on your previous interviews to ensure all the information is accurate and what you remember or learned from previous two meetings.

This does not mean that you should not prepare for the third interview. Although third interviews may not be a drilling process, they can still be a challenge since elimination is still possible at this stage especially if the second interviewer is unsure about you. The reason for that is you are dealing with more senior and experienced individuals. They are very skilled about asking tough questions and challenging you on your decision making skills, your analytical capabilities and most importantly how you handle and perform under pressure. The key is to keep calm- do not get flustered, defensive or angry. They focus a lot at your body language and your facial expressions. They are like detectives.

Let us now discuss a few tips that can help you in the second and the third phase of the interview.

- Know your resume inside out. Make sure you have answers for any gaps in your schooling or your employment.

- Know why you want to work for this organization and why should they hire you.

- Know the name and title of the person who will be conducting the interview.

- Remember the name of the person who did the first and second interview. In many cases they will ask you "Who was your first interview with", "What had they talked about our company". They want to see if you were paying attention in your previous interviews and, whether you are good listener or not.

- In your first and second interviews, if there were questions which, you did not answer, make sure that you prepare the answers for them. Make sure that you have reviewed your notes from your previous interviews.

- Be cheerful, enthusiastic, confident, and communicative and listen well.

2. Group Interviews

Most of you may not be well aware of this format of the interview. This is becoming the preferred form of the interview in most of the companies in the present time. In this form of interview, a group of candidates are interviewed simultaneously by one or more interviewer; one will be making notes and observing you during the interview. The general trend is that a group of 5 to 6 candidates is interviewed by 1 or 2 interviewers. Here, the stress is on the interpersonal and leadership skills of the candidates. It is expected from the candidates that they participate in the discussion going on within the group. The interviewers observe the attentiveness, the swiftness and the ability of the candidate to put forward his point of view, and still retain his exclusiveness.

These interviews are indeed very challenging and thus, a candidate needs to take proper preparations, so that he does well in it.

Preparations:

In the Group Interviews, a candidate needs to show his street smartness a bit and also be as polite and as dominant as possible. Let us now discuss some of the points that a candidate needs to keep in mind to be successful in the Group Interviews.

- Again, dressing as an important factor, may better not be neglected. If there is a need, you can also go to the washroom to comb your hair, before entering the interview room. You will definitely feel better.

- You need to know the names of at least 2 or 3 persons of your group, who will be going in for the group interview. This is very essential, as you might need to address them during the interview, so that you can add or go against their points of view. Doing this actually by referring to their names, will always put you in an advantageous position. This will help you collect some very precious points in the interview.

- You need to practice speaking at your home or with your friends, before appear in the group interview. You need to be a good speaker; else it will be difficult for you to do well in this form of interview.

- As a candidate for the group interview, you need to be a confident speaker too. So, you must have the habit of carefully listening to what others are saying. If you do not listen properly, then you will not be able to reply to the comments in a suitable manner, and so, you will be loosing points in the interview.

- Having a proper and friendly disposition is very important in this interview. So, do not be rude either to the other candidates or with the interviewers, during the interview. That will lead to your possible rejection from the interview.

- Never involve yourself in an altercation or a debate with your fellow candidates. There may be difference of opinions; try to accept them, rather than loosing your temper.

3. Panel Interview

A panel interview is that type of interview, where there are more than one interviewer, taking the interview of a single candidate. This type of interview is very common in the bureaucratic circles. You may also face this type of interview, if you have applied for a managerial post in a multi national corporation. Generally, a panel consists of 4 to 6 members. The members of the panel are from various backgrounds and are more often than not, experts of their field. The members of the panel may belong to the fields of art, science, literature, public service, law, teaching, armed services, diplomatic services, etc. So, it is expected that the questions that the candidate will be facing, will also be on various subjects. A panel interview is basically the test of the general knowledge and the personality of the candidate. It is to be kept in mind that when one of the panel members is talking to the candidate; the other panel members will be keeping a close look on the body language and the facial expressions of the candidate.

Preparations:

Let us now see in brief, what are the points that a candidate appearing for a panel interview must remember, so that he can perform well in that interview.

- In a panel interview, you will be facing questions on various topics. So, you must brush up your general knowledge. You may put more stress on topics such as international news, national events, sports, entertainment, etc. This will help you tackle many questions.

- Be sure to gain some knowledge about the post you have applied and also about the company or the Government department, in which you have applied.

- Maintain a good posture while sitting in the interview room, as you will always be watched by one or more members of the panel.

- Try to have a confident body language and be confident in whatever you are saying.

- Do not try to bluff, if you are not confident about the answers. If you do not know the answers, it is better to tell the truth to the panel of interviewers and they may put forward an alternate question. But if you try to create an answer that you do not know, you will be caught in no time and that may lead to your disqualification or poor marks in the interview.

- Always wear a gentle smile on your lips, which will make you feel confident and will add to your personality.

- You must face the member of the panel who is asking you the questions at a particular point of time. It is also crucial that you have a proper eye contact with the person with whom you are interacting. Do not be shy while having eye contacts. If you have eye contacts while speaking, it shows that you are confident of what ever you are saying. This will help you score more points in the interview.

- You must always listen before answering any questions. Always avoid answering in the middle, when the question is incomplete, but the answer is known to you. Listen carefully to the complete question, opinion or views when one of the panel members are trying to convey something to you.

- And definitely remember to dress in a presentable manner, that is suited for the interview, in which you are about to appear.

4. Campus Interviews

The name very clearly suggests the form of this interview. These interviews are held in the campus of the educational and professional institutions. This form of interview has gained popularity since the late 1970s. In this form, the companies reach out to the campuses of various universities and other professional educational institutions, to select their future entry level employees from amongst the students of those particular institutions. In the last decade, it has been observed that campus interviews are also being held in non-professional educational institutions. The whole concept of the campus interviews is largely dependent on the industry and its requirement of a specific type of human resource.

The Campus Interviews are held in various ways, depending upon the industry for which the employees are to be selected. Generally it is a three level affair. The first level is of the general interview session, which is followed by a written or objective type test. The final level is of the one to one interview with the Human Resource Manager.

First Level:

The first level of the campus interview takes place in the campus of the educational institutions. In this level, all the candidates, who have applied for a specific post in a specific company, are called up by the representatives of that particular company. The representatives meet the candidates one by one and get to know about them. This is generally an information gathering round and very rarely anyone is eliminated from this round.

Preparation:

Let us now discuss a few points in brief, so that you can create a better impression in the first level of the Campus interview.

- You must be in a presentable dress and behave in a very descent manner, so that you can create a positive impression.

- Listen carefully to the queries that had been put before you, and then only answer.

- Try not to speak out of turn.

- Prepare yourself for questions related to your hobbies, choice of subjects, idols in life, ambitions, etc.

Second Level:

The second level of a campus interview is generally a written or objective test. Here, the candidates are tested on the knowledge about his own subject. So, it is very important to perform well in this level. A bad performance may end your chances of being employed by the company. You must ensure that you are very well prepared for this test. This test may be a written one, where you are expected to write out the answers to specific questions, within a definite period of time.

It can also be an objective test, where you will be given questions along with some choices. One of the choices is the correct answer and you are required to mark the correct answers.

Preparation:

If you can keep the following points in mind, you will definitely do well in the second level of the campus interview.

- You need to go through all the major portions of the syllabus, to ensure that you remember all the major points. The questions are generally set on the most elementary but important parts in your syllabus.

- If the test is of the written type, then it is always better to practice some diagrams and use them as and when required. This will increase your marks surely.

- For the objective type test, you need to be careful while reading the question and also while finding the correct answers to the questions. The options given with the questions are more often than not, very tricky. So, you need to be very cautious.

- Be calm and collected while giving the test, as your whole career depends on the performance of the test.

Third Level:

If you are able to cross the first and the second level of the campus interview, then you will be in the third level. This level generally takes place outside the campus, in the office of the company that you have applied to. Here you get to meet the human resource manager or someone having a similar designation. This is generally a one on one interview, where your life may be made, or dreams shattered. In this interview, you will be asked about your subject, your interest to join the company and also your knowledge of the company will be tested.

Preparation:

The third level of the campus interview is very crucial, as this will ensure whether you get the job or not. So, you need to be very careful in this level. The following points will surely benefit you in this level.

- Placing yourself in proper outfit and being well behaved are two important things that the interviewer will notice.

- You must brush up the relevant sections of your syllabus that is important for the job that you have applied for.

- Maintain eye contact while conversing with the interviewer.

- You must be able to solve any problems pertaining to practical situations that may be placed before you.

- Maintain your calm and confidence and do not get excited even if provoked by the interviewer.

- Answer in a soft voice, without shouting or raising your voice unnecessarily.

- Do your research on the company and know why you want to work for them.

5. Behavioral Interviews

Behavioral Interviews are very new form of interviewing that has been developed in the late 1970s and the early 1980s. The people behind the development of this type of interview are the industrial psychologists. In this kind of interview, an attempt is made to know the real person with the help of the past experiences and reactions that the candidate has gone through. The aim of this type of interview is to help the interviewer understand whether the candidate is suitable for the job that he has applied for, or not. In this form of interview, a candidate is asked questions related to the qualities, which are required for the post he has applied for. You will be asked to give examples from your past experiences, when you have been able to show case such qualities that are required for the job that you are planning to take up.

A candidate needs to be very careful, while appearing in a behavioral interview. He must be able to present the right instances from his life, which fits the qualities that are being asked for. This interview depends totally upon your past experiences and how well you can remember them and present them before your interviewer.

Preparation:

The behavioral interview is a very simple affair, if you keep the following points in mind. These will help you to be successful in your interview.

- The first thing that you need to do is take a pen and paper and jot down the qualities that you need to have, to do the job, that you have applied for.

- After you have jotted down the qualities, try and figure out a few instances from your life, that highlights those qualities in your personality. You may also write down those instances on a piece of paper, if you think it will help.

- Be prepared to face any questions on the instances that you may be presenting before the interviewer.

- Avoid lying to the interviewer at any stage. This may prove to be too costly for your career.

- Be very precise and specific while delivering the answers to the questions that are being asked by your interviewer.

6. Competency based Interviews

The competency based interviews have become a very common feature in the job hunting field. Most of the candidates now face this type of interview, as opposed to the traditional interviews. The competency based interviews are also known as structured interviews, as in this type of interview; the candidate has to face many structured questions that are targeted towards him. The aim of the competency based interview tries to peek into the past of the candidate and find out, if he has the competencies that are required to perform the job that he has applied for. Every job requires at least 4 to 6 competencies. It can be the power to handle stress, or the ability to take quick decisions. It can also be the ability to work in a team or to lead a team. The interviewer structures his questions based on these competencies and tries to ascertain if the candidate has those qualities or not.

The candidate is asked instances from his past and his reactions to certain events. He is also asked to justify the reactions that he had shown and if he wants to make any amendments to that.

Preparations:

The competency based interviews are indeed very challenging ones and requires a lot of concentration and presence of mind, to get you through. Let us discuss some points in brief, which will definitely benefit you in the competency based interviews.

- You need to know very clearly what the possible competencies are, that are required to perform the duties of the post that you have applied for.

- You need to recollect from your memory, the events and incidents in your life, through which you can show that you actually have those qualities and competencies that the interviewer is looking for.

- You need to prepare yourself on the possible situations and tasks that may be put forward to you by the interviewer. It is important to practice as many situations as possible, before going in for the interview. It will give you that extra bit of confidence that can make all the difference.

- Try not to create any imaginative situations, while answering the questions put forward by the interviewer. More often than not, the imaginative situations and reactions are not convincing enough.

- Try to be very attentive while the interview is going on. Listen carefully and completely, before answering any questions.

- Try to be calm, composed and confident in your behavior and approach, during the interview.

CHAPTER 5

HOW TO PREPARE FOR THE INTERVIEW

"The future belongs to those who prepare for it today." ~ Malcolm X

You received a phone call

Getting a call for an interview is exciting. In many cases, a person who has not been employed before this turns out to be an even more exciting experience. As a result some people get nervous and find themselves at a loss for words, which often leads them to loose their train of thoughts. The key is to stay calm and collective by controlling your excitement and listening to the caller properly to get the information correctly.

Now a day employers are conducting more telephone interviews or telephonic screenings especially for candidates who do not reside in the same city. During a telephonic interview, you have to sell yourself with your words and your voice. This can be both an advantage as well as an impediment depending on how you handle the call. If you are well prepared for such screening calls from your prospective employers then you can soon turn the table and mould the situation to your advantage.

What is the purpose of the call?

The purpose of the phone call is to screen you and to get a quick evaluation of you. What employers look for is, if you are still interested in working for the organization. You could have found another job since the time you have applied for a position.

They want to see by asking you some key questions whether you qualify for the positions or not. Before calling you the employer has already screened your resume. They might have some quick questions to ask you about yourself, your qualification and your availability.

Do's and Don'ts of Calls for Interview or Telephone Screenings

Speak in a Lucid and Enthusiastic Manner

Speak clearly and answer questions with courtesy and enthusiasm. For employers who have not met you yet, your voice tone and projection can tell a lot about you to them. If your voice sounds listless and unenthusiastic while talking about your prospective interview then that would project a negative image in the mind of the interviewer. Not only that, a note of anxiousness or frustration about something might be easily deciphered by your interviewer. So, you should always try to sound positive, friendly and collected. You should avoid giving any negative and self incriminating answers which might reduce the chances of landing the job.

After the interview is over, do remember to thank the caller and emphasize that you are excited about getting the call and that you are looking forward for the interview. Thus, after the phone conversation with your interviewer is over, you should take the initiative to add that attending this interview would be a very interesting opportunity for you, and that you would definitely be able to make some value addition to the job profile.

Don't be over-familiar and over Excited about the Interview Call

However, in order to sound positive and friendly you shouldn't make the cardinal mistake of sounding over-familiar or too excitable. Even if the interviewer initiates some small talk during the phone conversation, you should be quite cautious about not blabbering too much about something which is irrelevant to your job or prospective interview.

Short and succinct sentences are better understood over the phone than long winding monologues. If you keep this key point in mind during your interview call, it would give you more opportunity for a fruitful interchange of ideas between you and the interviewer and would help you to retain his interest in your words.

Stay Calm and Collected on a Surprise call

Take surprise interview calls in your stride and try to stay calm and collected during such calls. Even if the caller had called at an inopportune moment, may be in the midst of a meal or a conversation, try to excuse yourself and find a quiet corner where you can attend the call in a composed manner.

Telephones are quite sensitive to the cacophony of noise in the background, and hence it is recommended that you take refuge in a room which would have the least amount of background noise. Shouting your answers in the telephone while there is a TV blaring in the background or a child wailing at the top of his voice would be an inappropriate way to handle a professional conversation let alone a call for an interview.

Be Prepared with Pen and Paper

When you get a call for an interview try to find a pen and paper as quickly as possible and write down the gist of the conversation. If the interviewer tells you anything significant about the company policy then do note those points down, as they might be of great help when you actually face the interview.

During the course of the interview, if your interviewer is interrupted or called away from the phone due to any reason, note down the topics and facts that were under discussion. When he/she resumes the telephonic conversation you can help him to recapitulate, "Yes, we were discussing…" Your attentive gesture and eye for detail would surely be appreciated and it will set you apart from other interview candidates.

When you are allotted a specific time for an interview make sure you write it down, and confirm with the caller the time and the date again before you hung up; like- "So, it is Monday at 4pm, correct?" Ask the caller the full name of the person that you are going to meet with and write it down. It is a good approach when you go to the interview, and greet the person with his name and shake his hands saying something like this, "Good afternoon Jim, I am Steve. It is nice to meet you".

Don't Eat or Smoke during the Call

As mentioned earlier telephones can be quite sensitive to background noise, so, don't munch on something while attending your call for interview. This can be quite irritating to the interviewer. It is also recommended that you don't puff on cigarette while talking to your interviewer too; this is also against corporate protocol. Surely you would not think of munching on crisps or smoking a cigarette during a face to face interview? So, why attempt these things on a telephone screening?

Give Precise and Factual Answers

The interviewer might ask you a few questions before you are called for a direct interview. Never try to fabricate or fudge any answers because your interviewer might have already gone through your résumé once, and he might even double checked the facts and figures provided by you once he has ended the call. So, you should never lie or mislead the employer regarding anything which you cannot later validate with facts. However, at the same time you should avoid replying in "yes" or "no" to the question you might be asked. Substantiate any answer that you give with proper logic and facts. This would be an indication of your quick thinking and logical reasoning.

Find someone to attend your Calls for Interview in your Absence

It is important that if you have someone at home who will be answering the phone, that they take proper information down, such as- who called, from which company, the phone number and most importantly did they give you the message. It is a good idea to inform your house hold that you are looking for work and that you have applied to different places. Tell them that they should expect calls for you and that it is important they take down the messages properly. If no body is supposed to be at home during the day, make sure that you have an answering machine at home. If you have a cell phone, make sure your voice mail is set up properly and professionally.

Start doing your homework

When buying real estate property, the real estate agents mostly emphasize on LOCATION, LOCATION, and LOCATION of the property concerned. Similarly, when it comes to doing well in an interview, PREPARATION, PREPARATION, and PREPARATION should be your mantra. The more prepared you are the better are your chances of winning the interviewer to your side. If you go to your interview ill-prepared you will simply end up sounding shallow and incompetent. Your interviewers might end up thinking that you are not serious enough about your job.

We are going to talk more specifics about how to prepare better for an interview and what you need to do before going to any interview. The best way to prepare for pre-interview, actual interview and post-interview is to remember the 3Rs.

☐ *Research*

☐ *Rehearse.*

☐ *Review*

Research the company:

Researching about a prospective employer is of great importance. In many interview settings the interviewer will ask you "What do you know about our company?" He might even reframe his question and ask you "Why you want to work here?"

Many interviewee get simply flabbergasted when they face these types of questions during the interview because most of the times they have no idea or information about the companies they are applying for. This is a cardinal mistake any interviewee can commit. If the interviewer gets an inkling that you have not even bothered to know about the company you are planning to work with, this is going to cast a negative impact on your ability to perform well in the organization, as well as seriousness about your career.

It is for this reason that you need to do an extensive research on the company and the industry you are applying. Completely and accurately researching about the company before attending an interview would enable you to field any questions the interviewer might throw at you without any hesitation or anxiety. Even if you are appearing for an interview at a very short notice, your inability to glean information about the company would never be excused.

Why is it so important to research the company?

1. Proper research provides you with detailed knowledge about the company which in turn gives you confidence. Remember knowledge is power.

2. It helps you to understand the culture of the company and provides you an insight into the key company policies.

3. Introduces you to their mission and vision statements.

4. It provides you with an opportunity to decide whether you really work for that company or not. If during your research you find out some unsavory facts about the company then you can always decline to attend the interview.

5. This kind of research also helps you to find out about the new projects and the latest changes that had been ushered in the company.

6. Extensive research also enables you to gain proper understanding of the company's position in the market and find out about their key competitors. It also gives you information on how much importance the company places on competitive marketing, which in turn would help you to answer question about the marketing strategies of the company during the interview.

7. What is their financial standing- are they making or losing money? This in turn also helps you to decide whether you would prefer to join a company which is losing its financial credibility in the market.

8. What is their corporate social responsibility? Many companies participate in various types of social welfare programs and detailed research about the company would enable you to have a proper idea about the ethical stature of the company.

9. It helps you to ice break and build rapport with the interviewer. Nothing impresses the interviewer more than your interest and knowledge about the organization. If you do detailed

research about the company you will be able to ask questions about the organization in an informed way. This is turn would influence the style and mode of the interview which would be relaxed and conversational type, rather than being an interview simply of question and- answer type. This will help in marking a line of differentiation between you and the other interview candidates.

10. It aids you to understand the vital trends of the particular industry the company belongs to.

How to research the company:

1. One of the key ways to research about the company is talking to people who are in similar fields.

2. Interacting with the previous employees is another key way of researching about a company. They would provide you with a wide array of information about the company which you won't find in any public domain. They would be able to provide you with vital inputs about company policies. You will be able to accumulate information about the employee relation policies of the company by talking with previous employees.

3. You can also do extensive research about the company by visiting your local library. Try to find out articles in business publications and industry trade magazines which are specifically written on the company you are researching on.

4. Searching the internet is perhaps the most common and popular method of researching about a prospective employer. These are the following places you should browse through to find out detailed information about the company you would be attending the interview for.

☐ **Company's Website:** Scroll down the entire website of the company. Try to jot down the key features about the company which might help you to field tricky questions during the interview as well as ask pertinent questions to impress the interviewer. Try reading the "About Us" section of the company website with special care. This would enable you to glean maximum information about the company's strategic goals, special projects and new developments.

☐ **Annual financial Reports**: This would help you to get an idea about the true economic standing of the company.

☐ **Press releases:** Browsing through the various press releases of the company would help you to find out about the latest projects of the company as well as the newly launched products and services. This would in turn help you to answer stock interview questions such as "Why should we employ you?" If you are well aware about the products and services of the company, you can emphasize why the company's products and services interest you and how you can add value to them.

☐ **Industry news:** You can find out the opinion of the current and previous employees of the organization through corporate message boards. However, you should read quite a few blog postings to form a concrete opinion rather than taking one posting as valid information.

☐ **Stock performance:** Checking out the stock performance of the company is another important way to glean information about the financial stature of the company.

Words of caution: Not everything you read about your prospective employer in the web or discussion groups are 100% accurate. Often people do tend to exaggerate any industry rumors without having enough facts and figures to validate them. So, do research about your prospective employer, to boost up your know-how. But also remember to sift through the wide array of information available, and pick up only those key details which come from reliable sources and can be validated.

While attending the interview try not to harp on the negative facets of the company, if any, because this would quite naturally reduce the chances of landing the job.

However, it is not recommended that you behave obsequiously and completely ignore something of this sort if you think it needs to be clarified. The key is to have a balanced approach. You may put forward questions in the interview like "Your annual report shows you lost market share to your competitor, how is that going now?" This kind of questions would be positive enough not to sound too harsh about the company's financial tribulations, but at the same time would indicate your in-depth knowledge about the industry and the company.

The Day before the Interview

The day before the interview, ensure that you do some final important preparations. Some of the key things that you should do before the interview day are discussed below.

1. Carry an Additional Copy of your Resume

Ensure that you make a couple of additional copies of your cover letter and resume. Some recruiters actually will ask you "Do you have a copy of your resume for me?" They want to find out how prepared you are. Having an additional copy of your resume will make it easy for you to follow along with the interviewer which in turn would give you confidence to talk about your self and your accomplishments.

I have seen it many a time when a candidate does not bring an additional resume with them, and I ask them question about some information on their resume, they respond by saying "Can I see that?" Sometimes when I ask them questions on dates which are written on the resume, they say "Let me take a look, please". That is why it is very important that you carry an additional copy of resume which would enable you to take a glimpse at it and answer the interviewer's questions in a jiffy.

It is natural for people to get nervous during interviews because they are quite anxious to please and impress the interviewer and land the job.   Especially those candidates with a gap in their work history get quite stressed while trying to remember the dates that determine their tenure of working with different companies. These dates are important as they specify which year they left and which year they started with the next company.

All these awkward moments can be avoided if you have an additional copy of your resume. Thus, when your interviewer asks "Which year did you leave your first job?" you need not give them a blank and sheepish look or request them to let you have a look at your resume which you had submitted earlier. You can confidently check out your own copy of resume and give them a clear cut and factual answer.

2. Review the Job Descriptions in Detail

Try to read the job description time and again and try to find out exactly what the company would expect from you. Find out what duties they are looking for and for each duty you must come with an answer beforehand. You have to see how you qualify and what you have done in the past with these kinds of duties and what measurable success you had with them. Knowing about these duties expected out of you should form the actual basis of your answer. You should mould your past experiences in a way which would highlight your ability to perform those duties underscored in the job description.

3. Arrange for the Transport to your Interview Venue

Try to double-check the following things the day before the interview: How are you getting there on the day of the interview, have you arranged your ride or whether you are driving, fill your car with petrol, check your tires. If you are taking public transportation, whether you have the timetable for the bus, train etc, and whether you need to make any exchanges. This might sound simple but surprisingly lots of candidates show up late because of this.

Google the address and see how long it takes you to get there. Try to check for alternate routes if possible, just incase there are accidents or traffic jams on the conventional route on that particular day. If possible drive to the location, so that you know exactly how long it takes and where the location exactly is. You need to be relaxed when you get there and not be stressed and panicked.

Taking care of the mundane details would ensure that you never turn up late for an interview. If you get hassled and harried just before an interview because of a punctured tire of your car, this would inevitably have an impact on your performance in the interview. You must remember that you need to be calm and composed to give the interview your best shot.

4. Take Care of the Personal Chores

Have your clothes ready and decide your attire for your interview before hand. You cannot afford to dilly-dally on the day of the interview just thinking about whether you are going to wear suite or casual dress for the interview. Get you interview dress washed and ironed and set to go. Make sure you feel comfortable in what you will be wearing. It would be useless to wear a three piece suit on a hot and humid day which would add to your discomfiture during the interview.

Go to bed early and get a good night's sleep, so that you can get enough rest and be fresh in the morning. If you are well-rested you will able to concentrate on the interview properly. On the other hand if you have had a stressful and sleepless night then it might make you appear listless and unenthusiastic in front of the interviewer.

5. Review and Rehearse

It is vital that you review the possible question that the interviewer might ask you just before the interview. Reviewing some of the key questions that might be asked on the interview would boost your confidence. More of this next chapter. If possible do a mock rehearsal of the interview in front of the mirror or with a friend or family member. Prepare the questions which you will be asking the interviewer during the interview. Prepare your references on a single typed sheet. Find out who will be interviewing you- their name and position. This will help you to break the ice during the interview and show how organized and prepared you are for the interview.

If you take care of these things the day before the interview, this would surely augment your performance during the interview manifold.

On the day of the interview

- Make sure that you arrive at least 15-20 minutes before your scheduled time. This is the first impression you will be giving to the prospective employer. Arriving early will also give you the chance to visit the restroom, check your appearance and go over your resume, review the advertisement which made you apply for the job, collect you thoughts and review the company history one more time. In other words, you will be more in control of yourself and would be totally ready to face the music.

- Avoid chewing gums during the interview. Chewing on a gum or a toffee during an interview goes against interview protocol.

- Do not smoke at least couple of hours before the interview. Your interviewer might turn out to be a non-smoker and strong tobacco smell emanating from you might turn him off. You should also avoid eating foods which have a strong smells at least a couple of hours before the interview too. To eliminate any chances of strong smells emanating from your mouth while you talk.

- Do not put on strong perfume or cologne when you go to attend an interview. Some people are allergic to strong smells and your interviewer might find your strong perfume or cologne too overpowering. That is why you should use light colognes or perfumes during interviews.

- Relax, reflect and reassure yourself that you are ready to face the toughest question during the interview. Just have faith in yourself and you will do fine.

Let the Show Begin

When the moment of truth arrives, it is important that you rise to the occasion and the challenge. After all, this is what you have being preparing for and dreaming about. The first few seconds of the interview when your eye makes first contact with the interviewer, is very critical. This is your chance to make your first impression and start on the right or wrong foot. It is important that you show confidence and enthusiasm.

As an interviewer at times I make up my mind in the first 60 seconds, whether I will likely or not likely hire an individual. Here is a real life example of a candidate I met, shook hands with to introduce my self, and walked towards the interview room. As I walked, I casually asked-

"How was your drive here?" And the response that I get at times is like this- "Oh, terrible the traffic was bad and rainy plus some people don't know how to drive".

Well what do you think I am thinking about hiring this person? What kind of attitude does this person have? Instead of giving the above response, what do you think would have been my reaction to thoughts about this person, if the candidate would have responded to the same question by stating "No problems, I took my time; and the instruction that you gave me on how to get here was great". You be the judge which candidate would you more likely hire. Your opinion is quite obvious isn't it?

Of course, after hearing the first response I thought that this kind of whiny attitude was indicative of the weak and intolerant character of the interviewee. I consequently decided that he would never make a valuable asset for the organization. On the other hand if the interviewee would have provided me with a positive response, it would have surely impressed me because I would have appreciated the candidate's ability to follow instructions correctly and his eye for details.

Thus, as an interviewee you should remember that first impressions often turn out to be the last impression. So, in order to have a lasting and positive impact on the interviewer you should put your right step forward from the very beginning of the interview. Not only your interview answers, but even your body language also can create an impression about you. The way you talk or the way you shake the interviewer's hand can tell a lot about you. You would surely not want to create a negative impression about yourself. So, keep in mind the certain key factors while attending an interview.

In order to start the interview on the right track, you should ensure that you do the following things when you meet the interviewer.

☐ Smile.

☐ Have a firm hand shake.

☐ Introduce yourself.

☐ Thank the interviewer for taking the time to meet you.

☐ Ice break by complementing the environment or commenting on something that catches your eyes.

☐ Never sit until you are offered a seat. Don't sit too close as personal space is important.

☐ Establish good eye contact with the interviewer.

☐ Be enthusiastic and positive.

☐ Do not fidget, keep your body in check (more of this in future chapter).

☐ Listen attentively.

☐ Speak clearly.

☐ Don't ramble.

☐ Keep your answers short and concise.

☐ Give examples.

☐ Avoid answering questions with just "Yes" or "No."

☐ Request clarification if you don't understand.

As you can see, preparing for an interview requires quite an amount of research and hard work. As stated earlier, the key to success in an interview lies in sound preparation. . So, the trick is to be methodical and organized and cover all your bases before you face the interviewer.

If you keep these simple criterions in mind while attending an interview you will surely be rewarded with the sweet fruits of your success.

CHAPTER 6

ANSWERING QUESTIONS DURING INTERVIEW

"Everything is difficult until it becomes habit."
~ Unknown

Answering questions, especially tough ones, during the interview is the most important part of the interview. Your answers will determine whether you will clinch the job or wait for another interview.

Many employers like to hire people who are not just qualified academically but people who have something extra. This is to ensure that their companies have the top caliber of brains that society can offer. For this reason, we take the process of interviewing candidates for various jobs to the next level. Through difficult questions we can cut out the unsuitable candidates and retain only those who seem to have an extra edge in them. All interviewees therefore need to brace themselves for difficult questions during interviews.

At all times, it is good to keep in mind that interviewers are not merely looking for correct answers but they also minutely observe the way answers are delivered. For this reason, no question should aggravate you and make you nervous. Even if you have no idea, you need to structure your words in a calm, composed manner and this will definitely be a plus. If you are able to answer even the toughest question in a composed manner, this would highlight the fact that you have enough presence of mind to tackle difficult situations and come out of those situations as a winner.

So, if you are faced with a tough interview question, which is totally out of your purview of knowledge, try to form an answer based on a generic logical reasoning and answer promptly. Do not hesitate to answer questions. This will show your incompetence and indecisiveness. Do not beat about the bush saying nothing; do your best and leave it at that. If you beat around the bush or simply keep mum, this might indicate to the interviewer that you might simply buckle under pressure in stressful or trying situations.

The following are practical pointers that will guide you into answering questions in a winning manner at an interview to land that dream job.

Rehearse

To do well in answering questions you must anticipate the questions that you will be asked. You must rehearse them so that they flow naturally during the interview. Remember interviewing is the process of selling yourself as a product to the interviewer. You have to highlight your best facets and key strengths in the least possible time. You really cannot change your experience or academic credentials, but what you can do is to highlight your strengths and downplay your weaknesses. The best way to do this is to practice time and again, the art of impressing the interviewer with your knowledge and panache. Do you know any actor who acts well but doesn't rehearse his lines? The best way to rehearse your answers is to do the following.

- **Write your answers Down:** You should glance through all the requirements for the job profile and write them down next to each key requirement, what skills and/or experience you have that is relevant. This would ensure that you are able to harp on these relevant skill sets and experiences during your interview.

- **Practice Aloud**: Practicing aloud would help you to get rid of any discomfiture that you might face during public speaking.

- **Mock Interviews:** Conduct mock interviews where someone asks you questions and another person observes your answers and behavior. This kind of role playing with friend and family members may highlight any flaw in your way of speaking or conducting yourself, which you might have missed. Somebody else might have any valuable suggestion to make about your speech pattern, body language or the answers you are preparing for the interview.

Know yourself:

Rehearsing will help you to know yourself. By preparing your answers well in advance and rehearsing them time and again, you would be able to ensure that you fully capitalize on your positives.

Use the S.W.O.T method to practice rehearsing for the interviews. S.W.OT is the acronym for

- Strength
- Weakness
- Opportunity
- Threat

Strength

An honest and objective self assessment is the stepping stone of the process of communicating your strengths during an interview. You should know your strengths very well.

One of the common questions asked during an interview is "Tell me, what your strengths are?" In order to answer this question in an impeccable manner, you should make an honest evaluation your personal qualities, skills and abilities and formulate your possible interview answer based on these. You should always endeavor to prove how you would be a valuable asset to the organization.

Some people answer this question by rambling on a list of qualities they have without having any clear-cut idea about how to sell these strengths. You do not need to ramble on a list of positive qualities, it is better to focus on three or four strengths and back them up with evidence. Your strengths should be based on what is on your resume. Some examples of strengths are your education, work experience, leadership skills and ability to work under pressure. Whatever may be your key strengths you should always validate them with logical examples and detailed facts.

Sometimes the interviewer might further confuse you by asking "Why should we hire you?" or he might rephrase his question in another way, adding "Why do you think you are the best candidate for this job?" These types of questions are also aimed at finding your positive qualities and your ability to make some value addition to the organization you wish to join. All these questions would have similar answers which should harp on your positive features and vital strengths as prospective candidate. The way you answer these question would make the crucial difference between you and the other candidates.

For example you can answer your leadership strength by saying something like "Due to my experience and ability to learn things quickly, I was the go-person whenever new training materials were introduced. People would come to me for answers and I would always provide brief summary for the team to make things easier."

To emphasize your ability to work under pressure you might even describe a particular difficult and trying project that you might have undertaken in the past. You could say "Our Company got a huge overseas project which had to be delivered within two months. I was able to motivate my team members so that they felt totally involved and ensured that they had the opportunity to contribute to the tasks facing the team. I was able to successfully deliver that key project within that tight deadline. I had to put in an extra bit of effort for the project and burned midnight oil but the client was happy with the quality of work".

If you are applying for the position of a manager you could also harp on your good communication skills and your ability to motivate others towards giving a better performance. Try to give some concrete examples like "I was able to encourage my staff to undertake some cost cutting measures which in turn helped to increase the profit figures."

Another great way of elucidating your positive qualities can be something like this, "I always actively participated in company presentations and workshops. I was also responsible for imparting training to new joiners. My communication skills help me to stand up and delineate my views in front of a group of people". Stressing on transferable skills like this is quite essential because companies always try to out for quality employees who would augment the development of the workforce.

Weaknesses

Similarly, another popular question during the interview is "Tell me about your weaknesses?" This is one of the trickier questions that might be posed towards you during an interview. If you answer that with straight-laced honesty and list your weakness, you might just prove that you are just not capable of doing the job properly. You need to answer these questions in a way which would neutralize your negatives and yet sound honest enough. However, most interview candidates don't bother to prepare themselves for this kind of questions. When it comes to questions like this, people can be divided into two **categories.**

People who don't know their Weaknesses

When this kind of question about the interviewee's weakness is asked, in many cases, the room is filled with a silence. Sometimes the room remains silent for a short period and at times the uncomfortable silence stretches for an extended period as the candidate remains totally flabbergasted. People simply get shocked when the interviewer asks them this particular question. Unwittingly their bodies betray defensive gestures. Most of the time, their arms gets crossed or their faces betray a certain nervousness or bafflement. **You can see they are feeling uncomfortable with the question**. Some candidates reply outright that "I have no weaknesses". If I face this kind of lackadaisical answer, usually, I reply with "So you are perfect?" This kind of inability to judge oneself is unpardonable in a prospective candidate and they usually have to feel the heat when they provide an interviewer with such shallow answers.

People Who know their Weakness and List them the Wrong Way

The second group of interviewees who are aware of their weakness don't fare any better in the interview. Infact, the way they enlist their weaknesses often cost them the job. Some candidates reply to this question by saying "I am a shy Person". Some others add that, "I lack self confidence at times". Some other stock answers include replies like "I get flustered under pressure", "I take things personally" or my favorite "I don't take criticism well". These answers might seem so naïve and funny, but these are all true and real answers that I get from some candidates. If you have listed your weaknesses in past interviews in a similar manner then you must now know how naïve and ungainly your answers might have sounded to the interviewer. This kind of answers would have definitely disqualified you as an eligible candidate in the eyes of your interviewer. So, it's high time to ask your self how you would answer this question.

However, the question remains how you should attempt to answer these tricky questions on weakness without jeopardizing your chances of landing the job. The best way to approach this is to:

1. Identify your weaknesses and make it relate to the job you are applying for. For example one weakness could be that you do not have a good job experience, or you did not complete the diploma you started, or you do not have enough computer skills for the job.

2. Focus on weaknesses which was an issue in the past and how, what you did to overcome them. This shows you are progressive and focused on developing your self.

Here are some of the responses one might consider in answering questions on weaknesses. If your interviewer questions you on your inability to finish your diploma course then you can formulate your answer on this following example. You could say, "I completed one year of the diploma with 80% average, however due to circumstances beyond my control I had to stop before I could sit for my final exams. I recently found out that I can complete the program through an online program which I will be starting in up coming September"

Focusing on weaknesses you worked on, will be by saying "In my last performance appraisal I was told I can improve on my planning skills. So, what I did I purchased a planner and used it on daily bases to get my self organized up on short term and long term objectives and I also read a self help book on planning. My planning is no longer a weakness and I am much more productive now".

However, there are some interviewees who try to act too smart while answering this kind of question about their weaknesses. While answering this kind of questions, you should never try to mask your strengths as weaknesses. Clichés like "I am a perfectionist and that is my weakness" would surely fail to impress an experienced interviewer and they would know instantly that you are feeding them a line.

Admitting a real weakness but then emphasizing your efforts to improve yourself would be much more appreciated by your interviewer. For example, you can say. "My communication skills were not as strong as I'd like and I was having some problem communicating with my clients. So, I enrolled with weekend communication skills classes and now I think I can communicate with clients much better." If you mention a weakness such as your impatience with people who don't do their share of the work, you should be cautious enough to also point out that you keep this impatience to yourself and always strive hard not to express it toward others in a harsh manner.

Strength and weaknesses are internal characteristic of a person which means it is part of you. Your negative facets remain an integral part of your character as your positive strengths. However, you have to highlight how you have endeavored and succeeded in overcoming your weakness. This would in fact emphasize your correct self assessment ability and your ability to learn from your mistakes

Opportunities

Opportunities are positive effects that might impact you and your carrier advancement, and increases your marketability if it is completed. For example you may highlight a new certification program which will be offered in the very near future that might be helpful to the employer you are interviewing with. You might say "I will be taking up the new certification which will be offered by Microsoft on Excel program which will help me tremendously in this job."

Often the interviewer might also take the SWOT method of questioning during an interview and ask you "What opportunities do you foresee for yourself in this job? Then you have to take a slightly different approach and underscore those opportunities that working in that particular organization might provide you with.

However, don't merely harp on the financial benefits of the job; try to state something else too. Many companies often sponsor their employees on part time MBA courses. You can add, "I am sure that I would be able to make some value addition to this organization but at the same time this organization can also help in materializing my dream of doing my MBA." So, you should clearly emphasize why you want this job and try to highlight how this relates to your future plans. You should also strive to clarify how this job aligns to your projected career trajectory and what you want to learn from it.

If you have applied for a job in a Multinational company you could even say, "While working with this organization I would get the opportunity with international customers which would enable me to learn new cultures and get accustomed with newer ways of working. This in turn would further aid me to provide top-notch customized services to my valuable customers."

Threats

Every organization wants employees who are not mere zombies but who can think on their feet. Ability to work under pressure situations and trouble shooting abilities are always appreciated by employers. That is why it is quite natural that the interviewer would try to find out whether you have the ability to handle and tackle challenges. So, you can expect the interviewer to ask you question like. "What threats can you identify in the job that is being offered to you and please explain how do you plan to tackle them?"

Almost everyone faces some threat or challenges at our workplaces but in order to have a prospering career you need to know how to survive with them. So, while talking about job 'threats' you would try to anticipate those challenges and problems that you might face at your prospective job and at the same time try to find out ingenious solution to those problems too. For example, "I know my role as the Public Relations manager of this company might require me to tackle multiple clients and this would in turn mean working long hours and overworking myself by taking so many responsibilities. I would try to put my time management skills to use to avoid getting overworked."

In order to answer this sort of question you need to do an extensive research not only on the organization you are applying for a job but also on the industry which you plan to work on. For example, if you have applied for a job of a bank manager, you can answer "Since the recession has cast a pall of gloom over the entire banking industry, maintaining huge overhead expenses and trying to regain our footing from the losses incurred is a big threat we face. If I am offered a job as a bank manager, I would try to enhance the profitability by emphasizing on effective cost cutting".

How to answer Behavioral questions

In chapter 4 we talked about behavioral interview style. As was mentioned, this style of questioning is becoming extremely important and is the most commonly used method in interview. This type of questioning is the most difficult one to answer during an interview specially if you are not prepared and rehearsed. The S.W.O.T system which we talked about earlier is the most common and traditional method of interviewing, in which a candidate can do extremely well specially if they are interviewed by inexperienced hiring managers. In this system it is easy to lie and you don't have to prove much of what you had said or done.

Nothing is more shocking for a candidate who thinks he is prepared for an interview ,and without any warnings gets asked a question like " Tell me about a project that you failed in and what was the out come?" or "Talk to me about a major contribution you did and why?". These kinds of questions can stop anyone on their tracks, if they are not prepared and rehearsed. So how do you answer these questions effectively?

S.T.A.R

S.T.A.R method is the best way to respond to behavioral questions. STAR is the Acronym for-

- Situation
- Task
- Action
- Result

Situation or (Task): When you are faced with a behavioral type of interview question, don't get flabbergasted. Begin with describing the situation in factual and succinct way. Then go on to describe the specific tasks that you carried out. You should concentrate and talk specifically about your own situation, and do not ramble on about other irrelevant issues. You should also not generalize while explaining your situation and task. Example you can say something like this, "As a manager of a sales team I faced deep problem due to a Drop in sales of vacuums by 2%. I was given the task to come up with a plan to augment the sales figures"

Action: After depicting your situation and task, you should move on to describe exactly what you did and how you did it. Needless to say, here also you should make your answers short and crisp and harp on your trouble shooting and problem solving abilities. You should frame your answers in a way that the interviewer is easily able to analyze your critical thinking ability.

Your aim should be to let the interviewer visualize how your method of thinking enabled you to get the team involved and how you solved the problems you faced. That is why you can add something like "I planned and organized a department meeting and trained all the associates on how to sell better and specifically emphasized on how to overcome customers' objections".

Results: As the time tested adage goes "The end justifies the means" That's why it is advisable for you to stress on what was the outcome of your efforts. Results are what people are the most interested to see, and hence you should clearly underscore how you were rewarded with the fruits of your labor. Thus, to complete your answer, you say something like "My newly implemented sales techniques improved sales of vacuums by 10%".

The outcome of your results can be organizational or personal. Organizational outcome is something which impacts the total employee base of the organization, or may be has an impact on the profits and business of the organization. To stress on these kind of organizational outcome, you can elucidate on a topic like this, like

"I implemented a new coupon system to help increase the sales in technical services department. My initiative offered customers $20 off coupon. As a result the sales improved by 7%". Or you can add something like this "As a sales manager of green appliances company, I devised a new training module for the sales team. This module harped on the ways in which our newly launched products can help people save money on electricity bills. This helped to augment our sales figures by 4%."

The personal outcome can be like improvement in your organizational skills, motivational skills relating to team work, leadership skills or knowledge based were you became much better implementer. An example will be like 'In setting up a new office I had to lead a team of 4 coworkers. I established my leadership very quickly by taking control of the project, and came up with a plan. As a result, we finished the work two days ahead of schedule".

The S.T.A.R method works the best when you make it sound as a good story. Are you a good story teller or not. If you are not then you need to practice these principles more and more by writing your stories on paper and then rehearsing them. The questions which might be asked in behavioral interviews are unlimited and it is not possible for any one to know the answer to all the questions; however the patterns are the same. The best advice will be to prepare four or five situations which deals with positive and negative outcome for each and use these answers to apply to any questions you might asked.

Examples of Situations with Positive Outcomes:

While describing those situations with positive outcome, you should be careful about harping on those situations which display your inherent skills and experiences in the best light. That is why while preparing for the interview; you should use your judgment and logic to choose those situations which would be a true testimony to your positive qualities. However, you should not be over the top while eulogizing yourself. Your tone and way of describing these situations should be quite matter of fact, yet compelling.

You might be asked- "Give me an example of a time when you motivated others". A question like this can be answered with a situation like the following one "I worked in the ordering department of our company. When a new product was launched I requested the management to provide me with a training module which was given to the sales team. I had known, knowing more about this product would help me to do my job better. I also motivated my team members to do the same. We receive excellent feed back from our customer for our in-depth knowledge of the different variants of the new product",

You might be asked- "Give me an example of when you showed initiative and helped the organization". The answer to this kind of question may be something like this- "I am responsible for ordering the stationary supplies for my company. I researched and found out that we could do quite a lot of cost cutting, if we bought stationary for the next six months all together instead of only ordering a month's stationary as is the usual practice. I did just that, and received an extensive discount for buying such huge volume of stationary. Not only did the prices of those stationary article rose within the next few months, I was quite appreciated for taking this initiative and ordering bulk stationary for the next sixth months."

Most organizations don't want their employees to be recluses. They want them to get along with other and increase the productivity of the organization by displaying team spirit. They don't want their employees to be Lone Rangers, rather they appreciate those employees who are able to adapt themselves to the company's environment and spirit quite easily, and become true team members. So, during your interview you can expect question like this, "Tell us about a situation in the past where you were able to display the spirit of teamwork.

If you are faced with such a situation, you should try to come up with an answer like this "I was part of the software implementation team in my last organization. We had to deliver a difficult software implementation project within a short time to a client who had the reputation of being quite strict about delivery schedules.

All the members of this team coordinated together to formulate an implementation schedule which was suitable for everyone and also ensured smooth and flawless transition for our clients. We had regular team meeting to keep each other updated and keep track of our overall work progress. By taking everybody in our stride out time, we were always able to deliver our project ahead of schedule. We received a positive feedback from our client too"

Examples of Situations with Apparently Negative Outcomes:

These examples apparently stress on those situations that are the negative outcome of your past experiences. However, you should also use these situations to subtly hint, how you later found a solution to that negative process. The interviewer asks this sort of questions to ensure that you have the ability to take defeats and difficulties in your stride and keep on striving to achieve a positive outcome. These sorts of questions about negative outcomes in past projects and assignments should thus harp on those failures you faced, but at the same time emphasize how you turned those failures into successes with your grit and determination.

The way you formulate these answers is of key importance. While answering these questions about your past failures you shouldn't allow your voice to betray any frustration or bitterness which might be remnants of your past dejections. Rather you should enthusiastically harp on how at the end you were able to get rid of those frustrating situations with your own hard work and ingenuity.

The interviewer might ask you "Tell me about a time when you missed an obvious solution to a problem?" This is quite a tricky question. However, you might come up with an answer like this, "I was at the manager of a retail outlet and every day I used to get bogged down with complaints about late deliveries. I couldn't figure out the problem initially, but then I found out that the problem was with the ordering department who were not informing the suppliers about depleted stocks in time. However after some extensive research, I rectified this problem and a follow-up system for the ordering department was implemented. Since the ordering department followed up with the suppliers and the stock problem was sorted the delivery team could in turn meet their deadlines too."

If you are asked" Tell me about a time when you were forced to make an unpopular decision", then you can harp on an unpopular decision that you took which was for the greater good. You can add something like this "As a manager, I found out that the work-desks of employees' were often quite messy with food stuff and spilled beverages. I mandated no food stuff could be carried to the work stations. This was initially quite unpopular with my staff but soon they also understood the benefits of having a cleaner office; and they themselves then took initiative to keep their work stations spick and span".

Some times the interviewer would try to check out your composure by asking such questions as "Tell me about an incident when you received a negative feed back from a customer or client". You can tell that "Since I had worked as a customer care executive, I had once faced flak from a customer due to a delay in registering her complaint. It was quite an embarrassing situation since the customer got quite incensed with my slow response to her request. I was partly at fault, since I was bogged down with a lot of customer calls and chores that day. I apologized to her and ensured that her complaint would get registered instantly. I also gave her a refund for the things she wanted to return. She remained a loyal customer of the store even after that incident and retained cordial terms with me. "

With an answer like this you would be able to harp that you didn't let personal ego interfere with your job duties. This would also highlight the fact to your interviewer that you can retain your composure in stressful situation and can handle criticism.

Thus, you can use these tricky behavioral interview questions to your best advantage if you answer them correctly. Judiciously use these tricky question to emphasize the fact that you are determined enough not to let minor set backs disappoint you, and you are ready to accept criticism to ensure your all round growth.

Review

It is critical for you to review and analyze each interview you go through. This will help you to identify the areas which you did well at and areas which you had challenge with. With an objective of self assessment and your interview skills, you would be able to detect your problem areas and work on them in future. That is why reviewing skills are of key importance in succeeding in an interview. As they say, failures are the pillars of success. This is applicable for interviews also. After you give an interview you should logically analyze every move of you make, and try to judge yourself objectively. Even if you are unable to land that particular job, this kind of deep insight and review would help you in other interviews.

However, you should not let yourself get dejected with failures. It is easy to get discouraged after a few rejections, but you should encourage yourself to stay optimistic about your job prospects and future interviews. If you suffer from depression or begin to nurture a pessimistic state of mind, this would infact hamper your prospects of landing a job. Changes in your mental behavior and your lack of self esteem will definitely show up as tell-tale signs in your body language which in turn can be detected by your next interviewer.

You must maintain your objectivity. If you are asked how your job search is going, don't show frustration, and do not mention that you have been applying endlessly and had many interviews with no luck. You should rather emphasize that your job search is going according to plan and that you have been selective as far as sending applications are concerned, since you are looking for a good match.

While we are talking about post interview reviews it should also be mentioned that in certain cases you might even mention whether you call up and know about the interview outcome. This sort of interest for a follow up to the interview would surely create a positive impression in the interviewer's mind. Even if you are not chosen for that particular position they might consider you, if any other opportunity turns up in the same organization.

CHAPTER 7

REFERENCING

"People forget how fast you did a job but they remember how well you did it." ~ Howard Newton

It is a norm to provide 3-4 references to your prospective employers who would testify to them about your experiences and abilities. Your résumé consists of words you wrote, trying to sell yourself, while references are the words of others' that can increase your salability in the job market. Surprisingly enough, very few people take references seriously. While creating your resume, you should devote considerable amount of time in picking your references.

Resume references can be a great marketing tool for your job prospect if they speak about you in glowing terms. However, during my years of experience as an interviewer and recruiter, there have been many cases where references have worked against individuals. Choosing an adverse reference would surely jeopardize a candidate's prospects of getting that job. That is surely an unfortunate situation when a deserving candidate is deprived of a job just because their references speak out adversely about their professional abilities.

That is why is imperative that you cross check with your references time and again before mentioning their names and contact numbers in your resume. The following are real life examples of how references have put deserving candidates in a disadvantaged position. Knowledge about these real life situations can help you to debar yourself from committing the same mistakes while picking up your resume references.

1. The candidate used a person as reference, who has fired him/her.

2. The candidate used a person as a reference, with whom he/she did not get along with.

3. The candidate did not get the permission of the person concerned, before using him/her as a reference.

4. The candidate gave an old, out of service phone number for a reference, that couldn't be reached.

5. The candidate gave an old supervisor's name as a reference, who no longer worked at that location.

6. The candidate gave the name of an organization as a reference that has a policy against giving references on grounds of privacy.

7. The candidate gave the name of a family member as a reference.

8. The candidate's job description on the résumé did not match up with the information of the references.

9. The candidate used a co-worker as a reference, who gave negative information.

10. The length of time indicated on the résumé did not match up with the references information.

11. The candidate gave their current place of employment as a reference, before informing them that they were planning to leave.

When you are asked to provide references, consider it to be good news. It means that you have passed the interviewing process and now you are on the short list of candidates to be picked for the job. You are normally required to provide 3-4 references.

Types of References

Any prospective employer usually asks for two types of references. These are as follows:

Professional Reference: Usually the employers ask for the contact number and contact details. The first one is of your previous or current supervisor/manager to be used as a reference. These kinds of references are known as professional references these references are usually used to judge and validate the professional credibility, experience and skills of a candidate.

Personal Reference: The second type of reference is the personal reference. In this type of personal reference you have to provide the contact details of a person from your personal acquaintances, who can vouch for your academic qualification. They can also testify towards your characteristic traits too.

However, many employers avoid using personal references as a base for hiring an applicant. The reason for that is, historically the outcome from hiring solely on personal reference has not been good. In many situations the candidates don't turn out at all to be what the person said on the reference call. The reason might be that since the personal references are often friend and acquaintances for the candidate, they are often reluctant to provide an objective feed back which might jeopardize his chances of landing the job.

In both cases the prospective employer is trying to find out and verify the information given by you on your application and résumé. Based on these findings the employer will try to make judgment about your behaviors, characteristics and traits.

Many employers do not like to give references. The reason for this is that it involves legality. If they say something very good about you and turns out to be not the truth, the new employer might sue the referring company, if you do something really bad. Secondly, if your previous employers give a bad reference about you, which causes you not to get the job and you find out about it, then they are afraid that you will sue them for slander, devaluation, character attack and opportunity of job loss.

Telephone Reference Checks:

Telephone reference checks are perhaps most commonly used method of reference checking. Some times references checks are also made through e-mails or letters. Since those processes are more time consuming, most employers prefer a direct telephonic interaction with the references.

To help you understand the most commonly asked questions during the reference checks, I have enlisted them in detail. If you are aware what kind of question your prospective employers might ask your references, it would help you to communicate this to the people who you are using as a reference. If you are using some one as a reference for a projective job, be sure to update them about the kind of questions that they may be asked. Some of the stock questions asked by the employers to resume references are enlisted below:

1. What can you tell me about the candidate?

2. What was the applicant's position when they left your company?

3. How much was he/she making?

4. Can you tell me 3 of the applicant's strengths and 3 of their weaknesses?

5. Did the applicant come to work on time?

6. How long did the applicant work for you?

7. Why did the applicant leave your company?

8. Was the applicant a good team player?

9. What kind of leadership skills does the applicant have?

10. Would you rehire the applicant?

Background Checks:

This method of reference checking is becoming more popular these days. The reason why this is becoming popular is:

1. Employers are hesitant to provide phone reference due to lawsuit issues.

2. Applicants are lying on their résumés about their jobs, education and using family members as references.

3. This style of referencing weeds out bad candidate once they know that background checks are involved.

Background check involve the applicant to sign a legal document in which allows the employer to check the background of the applicant for criminal offence, credit problems, bankruptcy claims, child support issues and work history. If you have any of these above mentioned problems and you come to know that your employer will be doing a background check then it is a good idea to come clean about the skeletons in your cupboard. If you have a bad credit history or have any felony charges in the past you should come up front and explain yourself before hand, so that your prospective employers don't get a nasty shock. If you appraise your prospective employer about any unsavory legal or financial hassles you might have had in the past, then they would appreciate you for your honesty at least.

If you are going to use personal reference as your main source for the employer then:

1. Don't use your best friend, as a reference.

2. Don't use a family member as a reference. No family member will give a bad reference.

3. Use your academic teacher or professor from school to be a reference.

4. Use your religious leader as a reference.

5. Use trustworthy past or current co-workers as a reference.

6. Use leaders of organizations that you are involved with or do volunteer work for.

Now you understand the importance of referencing. I am going to show you how you can best prepare yourself and your references for a potential phone call. This is what you need to do:

1. Inform your potential individual who you are going to be using as a reference that you would like to use them as a reference. Get their permission. Nothing is worse than getting an unexpected call. It is like a deer caught in a head light.

2. Have your list of references ready and typed. Have it with you in a separate folder when you go to the interview so that you

can provide it immediately to the prospective employer. This shows you are organized and prepared.

3. If you are going to be using former employers work numbers, call the number first to ensure it is the right number, and check to see if the person you are using for reference is still employed there or have they moved to a different branch or location.

4. Check in advance with previous employers to see if they will provide references to potential employers.

5. If you are going to use your current employer as a reference, make sure you let them know. Explaining to them why you are leaving or maybe you are looking for a second part time job to save money for school, making a big purchase or getting married.

6. Keep lines of communication open between you and your reference. People move around or change jobs. If they don't get any calls, that means your interviews are not working. Try to find out why.

7. Appreciate and thank your reference. Send them a thank you card or a gift, especially if you landed a job. You might need them again in the future.

8. Don't get them bombarded with phone calls. It affects their productivity and personal life. When they start getting too many calls, they might start having doubts about you and your ability to find a job.

9. What if you left the company in bad terms? You need to either find a different person to provide you with a reference or you have to meet with the supervisor and plead him/her how much you need them. You might also reach a mutual agreement with them to provide you with an answer that is acceptable to both of you. You might also like to get from

them a written reference which you can use to avoid a conflict with that organization.

However, there is another strategy you can use in order to avoid such unpleasant scenarios. If you worked for a company for a long time you must be aware of its official hierarchy. Each organization has different managerial levels, and the key is to find out a highly placed company official with whom you were in cordial terms. Try to find out the contact details of those managers or supervisors with whom you got along with the most. This method is much better than giving the reference of your immediate supervisor or reporting manager with whom you shared a difficult working relation and who in turn gave negative details about you.

It is important that you focus on your success, achievements and overall working relationships rather than on disappointments and failures. However, it is imperative that you should never criticize or bad-mouth an employer; this would really tarnish your image in the eyes of your prospective employers. Even if you had left your previous organization under difficult circumstances, and there have been lot of bad blood, you should always indicate that you left for a better job, improved conditions and for a more productive work environment.

CHAPTER 8

BODY LANGUAGE

"The body expresses what the mind is concerned with." ~ Unknown

The saying "A *picture is worth a thousand words*" should surely help you to get a true understanding of body language and nonverbal communication. As an interviewee you must ensure that your body language is saying the same thing as your verbal language. A good interviewer will be watching your non- verbal communication signals which come from the gestures and emotions which your body sends.

Some times these movements and gestures are consciously done while sometimes your body makes some unconscious expressions and movements which could reveal a lot about you. These gestures and expression would determine to a large extent whether you are communicating positively or effectively during the interview. For this reason, it is important that you understand at least the basics of body language to ensure success during interview.

To make things easier for you to understand, I am going to refresh your memory about different behaviors that you have seen from others or yourself. Think of a time when you saw someone angry. What did they do when they became angry? Did they put their hands on their hips? What does that mean? These non verbal gestures clearly indicate brute force and blatant antagonism.

I would provide you with another example. If you disagreed with someone when something uncomplimentary was being said about you, did you cross your arm? You did so because you became defensive and stopped listening to your criticism. Did you wiggle your finger at someone recently, did you role your eyes on some one when you were enraged. Wriggling your fingers at some one or rolling your eyes must have had much more effect on the person bearing the brunt of your temper more than your angry words would have had.

All these are example of non-verbal communication in which your gestures and feelings are speaking louder than words. All these gestures indicate your antagonism, irritation and defensiveness about the altercation or row you were having with someone. So, you can easily understand why it is important to control and manipulate your body movements and non-verbal communications while you attend an interview. By eliminating any negative non-verbal commutation and emphasizing on the positive gestures you can surely project the correct image to your interviewer.

Importance of Non-verbal Communication in an Interview

As per some recent surveys conducted by a scientific magazine, body language comprises 55% of the force of any response. On the other hand, the spoken words only provides 7%, of a forceful responses and rest of the 38% is comprised by the paralanguage which are the pauses and sighs given when answering.

Let us do an exercise as an example of non-verbal communication. Try to count till four starting with your *thumb*. Then you can repeat the same process starting from your *pinkie or little finger.* Did you notice the difference? Counting from the thumb indicates a forceful presentation compared to counting from the pinkie which is much softer or effeminate approach. This might provide an interviewer a glimpse into the strength of your character. You might give least importance on these gestures but you can rest assured that an experience interviewer would place immense importance not merely on what you say during the interview but also how you behave during the interview.

The notion that an evaluation of your non-verbal communication skills start when you face the questions of the interview is just a myth. The moment you enter the lobby of any organization till you leave the building after the interview every move you make would be observed and assessed as per the norms of non verbal communication. The way you greet the receptionist as well as the interviewer and the way you wait for the interview might as well have some impact on the whether you might be considered for the job or not.

Non- verbal communications during an interview is thus of quintessential importance for the interviewees. Your interviewer would definitely keep an eye on you to check out whether your non verbal communication throws up any hidden nuances of your character or not. Peter Drucker rightly commented *"The most important thing in communication is hearing what isn't said."* That is why it is all the more essential for you to glean information about what are the dos and don'ts of non verbal communication during interviews. This would ensure that you don't make a faux pas with your body language and dressing sense.

You should always try to remember that the first image that the interview has of you as a prospective candidate often lasts forever. If you appear messy, fidgety or sloppy to the interviewer, no matter how ingenious and well prepared your interview answers are you may never going to land the job. On the other hand your impeccable non-verbal communication, your firm hand shake, fine dressing sense and perfect behavior might just clinch the job for you.

Non-verbal communication is divided into few categories. Some of the key gestures and appearances which you should be aware of during interview are enlisted below.

- **Interview Attires**

- **Gestures and Postures**

- **Facial Expression**

- **Eye Movement**

- **Voice and Intonation**

- **Others**

Interview Attires

Mark Twain very aptly said **"The finest clothing made is a person's skin, but, of course, society demands something more than this"**. The way we dress can often tell a lot about us and hence as an interviewee you should pay minute attention to personal presentation at the interview. While dressing yourself up for the interview, your dress should understated enough to complement your credentials and skills, and not assume maximum attention, while being moderate and well-fitting. Lack of proper sense of dressing can break your interviewer's opinion about you, which might have been formed through your resume and credentials.

The way you dress during an interview can make or break your interviewer's opinion about you. Appropriate interview attire substantiates your image as a person who has taken the interview process sincerely and understands the nature of the industry he has applied for. As per a survey conducted by "*U.S.A Today*" magazine outlandishly dressing during an interview can cost you the job, however qualified you may be. While appearing for an interview you should avoid funky and overtly casual clothing. Try to avoid those kinds of baggy pants which hang too low on your hips. A stern interviewer might even reprimand you to "pull up your pants".

The situation might appear funny to you but believe me you would be considerably embarrassed and consternated by that. If you have conspicuous tattoos and body piercing then it would be prudent to wear clothes that might cover up those body tattoos and piercing. You might consider your tattoos quite cool but you have to remember that your interviewer might not share you funky fashion sense. That is why it's always better to play it safe.

Business-Casual Attires

The job you are applying for often should dictate the kind of apparel you should chose for an interview. If you are going for an interview in a store or warehouse formal attire would look incongruous. In such cases you can choose to wear business-casuals. Now days even if you are applying for a job in an advertising agency or may be in a software company then also you can afford to wear a business-casual dress. However, the term "business-casual" attire is quite a vague term. For different companies it might mean different things.

For some companies business-casuals might mean a polo neck shirt and jeans while for others it might mean ironed shirt and trousers or clean button down shirt and khaki trousers. If you have the opportunity to visit the office premise before you appear for an interview then you might notice what the company employees are wearing and dress accordingly. If you don't have that opportunity then it is better to avoid jeans and t-shirt and opt for khaki trousers and a buttoned down shirt.

If you are appearing for an interview in a law firm or in a bank it is better to opt for a suit or a jacket along with a tie for men and a skirt suit for women. Formal attire is always the safest bet while attending an interview.

Ramzi Karim

Gestures and Postures

Your body language and body posture conveys a lot about you to your interviewer. You should be aware of your correct body posture learn how to use it to emphasize a great image towards your interviewer. Gleaning information about body posture and body language would also allow you avoid those which might reduce your chances of being deemed as an ideal candidate.

Relaxed Body Posture

During an interview you should adopt a body posture which would portray your interest in the interview process and yet comes across and quite relaxed. When you are invited to take a seat, sit up straight and lean a little bit forward. This gesture would testify towards your keenness and attentiveness for the interview process. However when you are asked to take a seat in front of the interviewer you shouldn't sit too close to the interviewer, incase there isn't a table in between you. You should always keep at least 30-36 inches of gap between you and your interviewer because violating personal space is always considered rude.

Many interviewees feel quite nervous during the interview. Even if you are feeling nervous you shouldn't give that impression to the interviewer. You can effectively camouflage your nervousness through correct body posture. So, when you sit down in front of your interviewer you should not hold your upper body too taut; rather you should take a relaxed and comfortable posture when you sit awaiting the questions of the interviewer.

However, this doesn't mean that you should take the interview process too informally and get overzealous to prove your relaxed state. That is why it is always imperative you should never slouch on your chair when you face an interviewer. This might have a boomerang effect and might prove you as a nonchalant person who hardly cares for the interview process.

Open Gestures

Your chin should be out and don't cross your arms to show openness. Crossing your arms is always interpreted as a defensive gesture and it might indicate to the interviewer that you might have something to hide. Open gestures are always preferred over crossed ones, since they are more trusting and welcoming. While you nod in affirmation to something your interviewer says you should nod slowly. Nodding repeatedly while some one else speaks might stamp you as an impatient person and the interviewer might think that you are too eager too add your bit to the conversation.

Hand Movements

Many interviewees are quite at a loss as in where to place their hands while attending an interview. They consider their hands as an obstacle rather than a means of effective non verbal communication. Your hands should comfortably rest in your laps or the arms of the chair. Sit comfortably and don't move back and forth in your chair. Leaning forward a little bit or titling your head forward considered as a friendly and cordial gesture and indicates you want to learn more.

Nodding your head while speaking in an interview, is a key way of supporting your words with body movements. It might imbibe some force in your words. Hand movements can also be used to facilitate your conversation or emphasize your points but you should use hand movements sparingly.

You should not make too much hand movements from the very beginning. You should start making hand movements when the interview conversation grows animated and might need livening up. However, you should always avoid negative hand movements such as clasping the back of your head with your hand or rubbing the back of your neck with your hands. These might be considered as unreliable and self-protective gestures.

Facial expressions

The time tested adage proclaims that the face is the mirror of the soul and hence your facial expressions might reveal a lot to your interviewer. The interview always notices the facial expression of an interviewee with unusual care because an interviewee's face projects the emotions and feelings that are going through him. It is therefore vital for you to control your facial expressions during your interview and avoid displaying negative emotions such as anger and bitterness.

Even if an interviewer throws a question at you which you might consider rude or intrusive you should never arch your eye brows or scowl at him. You should be careful not to display any grim expression in your face which might indicate that you have taken affront to the questions that are being asked.

You should also not bite your lips if you are at a loss while answering a tricky interview question. This would indicate your baffled state. As mentioned in the earlier chapters, when faced with a tricky question you should gather your wits quickly and formulate a logical answer rather than deliberating over it time and again. The interview must not see you appear confused and flabbergasted because this might make him think that you don't have quick wittedness to tackle tricky situations.

While attending an interview your face would carry, show a pleasant and eager expression as it shows confidence and security. However, this doesn't mean that you have to paste a bright smile on your face through out the interview; it simply means that you should appear as a friendly and cordial person. If you paste a plastic smile in your face through out the interview that would in fact make your behavior artificial and simulated.

Eye Movements

Your eyes communicate a lot to the interviewers. Emerson has aptly commented *"The Eyes of men converses as much as their tongues."* It is crucial to maintain good steady eye contact with the interviewer in order to communicate confidence and trust. Your eyes start speaking about your level of confidence the moment you meet your interviewer.

Ensure Direct Eye Contact with the Interviewer

From the moment you shake your hand with your interviewer you should try to establish direct eye contact with him. As per the norms of non-verbal communication avoiding eye contact or being shifty eyed shows that one is not being truthful or is shy and timid. So, if you avoid direct eye contact with the interviewer when you meet him he might interpret you as a shady or untrustworthy character. On the other hand a direct eye contact with the interviewer would testify to your confident attitude.

If you are offered to choose a seat during your interview you should always chose a seat from where you can directly look at all the interviewers. You should sit directly facing the interviewers and look straight at them. Don't let your gaze stray on the pictures or decoration of the room for more than a while lest you might be branded as being unmindful. During a panel interview avoid staring at a particular interviewer and look at every one at equal extent.

Use your Eye Movements to Emphasize your Points

When your interviewer speaks on some important issue pertaining to the organization you should keep looking at him till he has finished speaking this would indicate your keen interest in whatever is being spoken about. While your interviewer speaks he might look at other people present in the room too but when he wants to harp an important point to you he might look back at you. You should nod or tilt your head in affirmation in order to encourage him to speak on. Rolling your eyes while listening to the words of an interviewer could indicate your inner frustration and might appear annoying to the interviewer. While speaking also eye movement can be used to emphasize your points.

When you start answering an interview question you should first look at the interviewer who had posed the question. During the course of your speech you might look at other interviewers too but when you want to emphasize a key point you should look back at the interviewer who asked you the question. While you end you answer you should again shift your eyes to the person who had questioned you. If you are wearing glasses you should never peer over your glasses because that might be considered as rude and arrogant gesture.

Voice and Intonation

The tone, pace and intonation of your speech during an interview is of crucial importance. Your voice should be well controlled and calm when you speak to your interviewer. While speaking to your interviewer you should not be too hurried or out of breath because that might reveal your nervousness to your interviewer. If you are really feeling too nervous to speak up in front of the interviewers then just take a couple of deep breaths when you start speaking up.

Let your Voice Depict your Enthusiasm

You should let your voice depict your animation and interest in your prospective job. So, while you speak you should not speak out in a droning monotone that might be interpreted as indicative of your disinterest in the interview and the job position being offered. Your voice should be clear and audible and enthusiastic. However you should also take care not to   raise your voice too much because that might be considered rude by your interviewers. Similarly, a sudden drop in intonation as opposed to a raising voice might also indicate a lack of interest in the topic being discussed by the interviewer.

If you want to have the perfect voice modulation and intonation during your interview then you should conduct several mock interviews before you appear for the real interview. Your friends and family with whom you participate in mock interviews would be able to guide you about your perfect voice pitch and voice modulation. During your mock interview tell your friend or family members to note whether you are speaking too fast or your voice is sounding too shrill. Then, as per their feed back you can make the necessary changes to your voice module.

A well modulated voice and a confident tone adds an extra edge to spoken words. As an interviewee you should remember that your diction, intonation voice tone everything has an impact on the interviewer. It is up to you to use these tools to reinforce your image as an ideal interview candidate.

Use Proper Diction

How you frame your words during an interview also holds quite a lot of importance. You should always use positive language during an interview. During your interview you should never let any negative emotion like anger or irritation overpower you because that would not merely change your facial expression but that might make your voice should harsh and coarse too.

You should also be careful about the diction you use during an interview. However, agitated or angry you might be during the course of an interview you should never ever use any profanity. This would definitely disqualify you as a prospective candidate for the job on offer. . Thus, while speaking with your interviewer try always avoid slang or colloquial diction. On the other hand use of fine diction would definitely help you to score a brownie point with your interviewer

Other Miscellaneous Factors of Non-Verbal Communication

When you walk into a room where the interview is being conducted try to walk in straight with your head held high. Stooping or slouching would definitely act against you. These are considered negative gestures and you should avoid them at all cost. When you shake your hand with the interviewer you handshake should be firm yet not bone crushing.

A sweaty and limp handshake might reveal your nervous state to your interviewer. Thus, even if you are quite anxious about your impending interview you should wipe your sweaty palm in a handkerchief before you go in to your interview room. This would ensure that when you shake the hands of your interviewer they are not repelled by your clammy hands. You should also avoid some negative gestures as playing with your hair or adjusting your tie or coat too much. These gestures might brand you as too frivolous or narcissistic.

While the interview is on you body language should never reveal your impatience or nervousness about the grueling interview rounds. Some body gestures like drumming your fingers against the table top, or fiddling with a pen or pencil could prove to be quite irritating to the interviewer.

These fidgety behaviors might indicate to him that you are too impatient or bored with the interview process. You should also never shuffle your feet during the interview or kick at the leg of the chair. These gestures would consider as restless and childish body postures which would surely be not indicative of your maturity and competence as a job candidate.

In order to command an impeccable and perfect body language during an interview you might have to put in a lot of effort. If you want to get your body language right then you can rehearse in front of a mirror or with a friend before going for an interview. Just remember not too come out as being too informal in your effort to appear calm and confident.

It is also important for you to observe the behavior of the interviewer if you see any of these gestures not being received well by your interviewer then you should take the hint and adjust and change course of your non verbal communication. For example, if you are gearing for an animated round of interview where you want to impress your interviewer with your enthusiastic body language and verbal proficiency.

However, if you feel that your interviewer's demeanor towards you is too cool, sedate and detached then you might tone down your animation and enthusiasm and appear a little more formal in your body language. On the other hand if you feel that your interviewer likes your enthusiastic and dynamic style of communication then you might intersperse your verbal speech with some greater intonation and hand movements.

So, ultimately it would depend on you to fine tune your body language or non verbal communication with your interviewer in a way that he is justly impressed. However, if you keep the above mentioned guidelines in mind you would surely succeed to make a positive impact on your interviewer with your body language and non-verbal communication skills.

CHAPTER 9

THIRTY COMMON INTERVIEW QUESTIONS AND ANSWERS

"A man is hidden under his tongue." ~ Imam Ali

In this chapter I will discuss some of the most popular questions which might be asked during an interview. I would also try to give you pertinent information on how to answer these key questions. It is worth emphasizing again that one must rehearse these answers time and again so that they flow naturally when you face the interview.

You need to keep your answers short but effective. When answering questions don't be mechanical; otherwise these answers would come across as memorized or scripted. You should retain your natural enthusiasm and zeal while answering these questions. That is where your facial expression and tonal modulation can help you. They can help to make your answers more convincing.

Before answering any of these questions take a couple of seconds to pause and collect your thoughts. This would really give your interviewer the impression that you are striving to frame your answers by trying to recollect relevant details from your work life or academic life. If you start parroting your answers the moment the interviewer asks them then he would really understand that you are merely reiterating something that you might have memorized. Thus, it is imperative that you never lose your ingenuity and quick thinking while answering these questions.

However, before elaborating on the common interview questions you might be asked and providing you with relevant clues about how to answer them, it is quite important to let you know about open-ended and close ended questions. Gleaning information about these types of questions would help you to formulate appropriate answers for them which would definitely woo your interviewer.

Open-ended Questions

An open-ended question is that type of interview question which provides the interviewee an opportunity to frame their response and elucidate it properly. Open-ended questions usually begin with "Who, what, when, why or how". For example, "What are your weaknesses?" or "What positive benefits do you expect to gain from the position being offered?" "Why do you wish to join our company?" "How would describe your work experience with your previous organization?" The list goes on and on. However, you must understand the purpose of these open-ended questions in order to answer them with flair and panache.

An interviewer asks you open-ended questions so that he can get to know you better without having to indulge in a conversation. An open-ended question provides you the opportunity to put your thoughts forward and speak up.

It is imperative that you answer each question as thoroughly as possible without rambling too much. You should stay focused and aim to highlight your accomplishments and strengths. Thus, while answering open ended questions you should give more than the facts and figures about your work experience and academic accomplishments.

Just remember that an interviewer would try to find out about the level of enthusiasm for the job and he would also try to determine if you would fit in properly with the corporate culture of that particular organization. So use these questions to tell more about yourself and give the interviewer a positive insight into your character. At the same time you should back up your answers with examples and reasons. Your examples and the answers might change the track of the interview and lead to more questions which might put further emphasis on your accomplishments. You should always try to achieve the aforementioned goal.

However open-ended questions also allow an interviewer to judge an interviewee's communication skills and hidden nuances much better than close-ended questions. So, you should be on your guard while answering these. Try to take some time before answering each question because you would be revealing facts about yourself and your work ethics which might also be detrimental to your job prospects. So, just pause and reiterate the answer in your mind before you blurt it out.

Close-ended Questions

A close-ended question is that kind of question which usually restricts the candidate to choose a particular and concrete answer. In other words close-ended questions usually elicit a "Yes" or "No" response Close-ended questions are usually framed like this: "Have you ever failed in a project?" How many years of experience do you have of working as a sales manager?" "Have you ever worked from home?" "During your stints as a marketing manager did you ever go with a sales representative on a direct meeting with the client?" This sort of questions allows the interviewer to take the full control of the interview.

An interviewer would ask you such questions when he wants a direct answer on some key issues and he wants to avoid any sort of prevarication. Close ended questions are used to uncover specific information about a candidate. Even if there are times when a simple "yes" or "no" answer is adequate most of the times you should also take up the chance to elaborate. Simple yes or no answers might not explain your situation properly.

It might even frustrate you if you are not able to give proper and relevant data while answering close-ended questions. However, you can simply rest assured even if the interviewer wants direct answers he doesn't want to end up as the one doing all the talking during the interview. So, you can always subtly add some explanations with close-ended questions too. That is why you should try to answer these close-ended questions as "Yes, but…" or "No, however…."

So, the next time you are faced with these open-ended and close-ended questions, try to don your thinking cap and answer each of them with due care keeping these aforementioned guidelines in mind.

Now, let's go and find out about some of the most common interview questions which you might expect your interviewer to ask you.

Common Interview Questions

1) Tell me about yourself:

This is the most commonly asked question in an interview, normally it is asked right at the beginning of the interview. Answering this question effectively will give your interviewer the impression about what kind of person you are. The best way to answer this question is to have a short sample answer prepared in your mind. You should ideally keep your answer related to your academic accomplishments and work experience unless the interviewer specially asks to fill in some personal details. You should list the key positions you have held in your work life and elaborate on the job responsibilities in you previous organizations.

However, you should try to structure you answer in such a way that it emphasizes your experience and eligibility for the job you are being interviewed for. You should start with your farthest experience in your resume and work up to the present. However, you should ensure that your answers don't become too long and boring. Answering this question should not take you more than two minutes.

You can come up with some thing like this "My back ground till date has motivated towards honing my skills to become one of the best sales managers in the industry. Let me tell you how I have prepared myself. I have graduated in Sales and Marketing from ... university. I also have experience of working as a sales trainee in ..... Organization where my job responsibilities involved interacting with the clients and attending sales meet. I also assisted the sales manager to prepare sales and marketing reports. I think both my educational qualification and past job experience have prepared me well to handle this job of a sales manager."

However, while answering this question don't go on rambling about your accomplishments. Your answers should be precise, factual yet effective.

2) Why do you want to work for us?

Some people come up with weirdest answers when asked this sort of questions. Some of my interview candidates even answer- "I applied for this job because I like people" This sort of simplistic answers are just too comical and childish to be considered appropriate for an interview candidate.

This question is easy to answer if you have done a thorough research about that particular organization in which you have gone for your interview. I have already stressed on the importance of research in the previous chapters. If you know the key details about the organization then try to harp on the long term benefits you can attain if you work for the organization.

Try to think of the unique facets of the company; how the company believes that it is different from its competitors. Try to incorporate these positive facets in your answers. If the company stresses on research and development try to include veneration for creating things in your interests and reasons for working in the company and say you would like to work for a company which encourages these creative streaks.

You can also stress on the opportunities that this particular job profile might offer you to materialize your long term career goals. You must however sound quite genuine when you show your enthusiasm for working for that organization. The interviewer must not feel that you are heaping false praises on the company just to secure the job, thus in this case sincerity should be your key to success.

You can frame something like this "My role as a sales manager in your organization would provide me the opportunity to handle international clients. I think that would be a great exposure for my career in sales." You can also talk about the various community efforts that the organization has undertaken and appreciate their corporate philosophy too as you clarify your motive for wanting to work for a winner.

3) Are you a team player?

While answering this key question don't just mutter a pithy "yes" and stop. Even if this is a close-ended question your interviewer would surely want you to substantiate your answer with precise facts. You need to give specific examples of situations in which you were an effective member of a team, what was your role and what were the out comes. You surely don't want to come across as a solo performer and a lone ranger that's why it's essential that you emphasize your team efforts properly.

You can say that "In my last organization, as a sales manager, I was responsible for coordinating the activities of the entire sales team. I was the one who arranged sales meets. I always ensured that all my team members were well coordinated with each other and we worked together to elevate the drooping sales graph of the company. As a result we could almost bring up the sales by 2%. "

4) Why would you think you will be an asset to our company?

The interviewer would ask you this kind of question because he wants to find out how you fit into the culture of the organization and what kind of relationship you will develop with other employees of the organization. This question gives you the best opportunity to showcase your strengths and positive points which are to the position you are applying for.

You should elaborate on your ability to understand, esteem, and function within various corporate culture. Try to site pertinent examples where you've proven yourself to be trustworthy, meticulous, and detailed-oriented. You should take this opportunity to use highly motivational words about yourself that will surely impress your interviewer. However, you should also be sure not to be too boastful and come across as a braggart.

5) What irritates you about your co-workers and your boss?

These types of provoking questions are meant to draw out your inner resentment and rancor and at any cost you should not speak anything ill about your supervisor, subordinates or coworkers. This question is surely a show stopper in an interview and you should answer this with due care.

The best way to answer is just making a short comment about yourself that you don't get irritated easily and you get along with people very well. This is the best way to emphasize your broadminded nature and your unwavering composure towards the trials and tribulations that you face in your job.

6) What is more important to you: the money or the work?

While answering this question don't try to trivialize either your work or your monetary requirements because both these criterions are equally important. Since you are looking for a job in a professional capacity it is expected you would give due importance to the financial aspects of a job. So don't try to act like a saint by commenting the remuneration of the job doesn't really matter to you.

You should rather stress that even though the commercial viability of the job often determines our job decision, having a congenial and effective work environment is also of great significance too. Thus, the best answer would be, "The money is important, but the work is the most important."

7) Tell me about a problem you had with a Manager.

This question is another booby trap for naïve interview candidates. This is a classic question asked to find out if you would speak negatively about a manager or supervisor. By asking these sorts of questions the interviewer seeks to ferret out information about your working relationships with your supervisors and managers.

If you take the bait and speak negatively, you might as well kiss the job goodbye. The best approach in answering this question is to stay positive and say that you have a poor memory about recalling any problems with supervisors. So, try to stay calm and composed when you hear this question and never blurt out any unpleasant incident which you might have had with your previous bosses. You can simply say, "I got along quite well with my previous managers. I can't recall any specific incident which deserves a mention in this regard."

8) What motivates you to do your best on the job?

Through this question the interviewer wants to know what motivates you and is also trying to find out about your personality. To answer this question well, it is best to focus by giving good examples on recognition, respect, challenge, winning attitude. You can say that you want to excel in your career and be recognized as one of the most competent people in the industry.

You should take this opportunity to harp your constant endeavor to earn the respect of others and your zeal to be a true winner. You can rest assured that the interviewer would be looking for an ambitious streak in you. He would try to ensure that you have enough ambitious zeal and professional fervor in you to do proper justice to your job responsibilities in future

9) Describe your management style

This is a very interesting question because everybody has different understanding and knowledge of management styles, and depending upon which expert you listen to, you might get a different meaning. However, your extensive research about the company you have applied for a job would help you to identify what kind of work environment and management style they prefer. If you already know about the management style of the company then make sure that your own ideas complement it. If you are totally unaware about their management approach then you can put forward one of the management approaches of your own. As they say different strokes go for different folks this is true while choosing your management approach too.

There are various types of management style prevalent currently like the progressive or open door management style which depends on motivating people and delegating work to right people. Then there is the result oriented management style, where the management decision taken decides how it would affect the bottom ranks of the company as well as its sales graph. However, one of the most effective and safest ways to impress the interviewer is to stick to the situational leadership style.

Every organization appreciates having some body in their team who would shoulder extra responsibility to steer the team in the right direction during the time of need. You can say something like, "I like challenges and trouble shooting. If the situation so demands I

---

can shoulder extra responsibility and help to guide my team mates to find an effective solution. I am ready to work hand in hand with them than just being a supervisor or manager."

10) If you were hiring a manager for this job, what would you look for?

This is another question which is quite difficult to handle. Many candidates just go overboard and try to elaborate on the particular qualities they have. However overtly blowing your own horn is not the right way to answer this question. You should focus on the job requirements which are stated in the job description and then carefully enlist the commensurate qualities and skills which you have. "You can say I would definitely hire some one who is capable of moving up in the organization with their initiative, hard work and relevant experiences about this retail industry."

This would clarify to the interviewer that you are well aware of what the job entails and you have the required qualities to succeed in the job. He would be also impressed with the fact that you are diligent and meticulous enough to have gleaned elaborate information about the various facets and nuances of the job you have applied for.

11) It seems you lack the experience, how would you compensate for that?

When faced with this kind of questions you must point out those facets of your job experience which might not have been mentioned in detail in your resume. However, if you are just a fresher being interviewed for your first job then you need to emphasize on your ability to learn quickly and your determination to succeed in your field despite all odds. If you are being interviewed for your first job you can also mention that even if you don't have experience of working as a full time employee you have other experiences and skills sets which you have gathered from your voluntary works. Thus, you should steer the conversation towards experiences and skill sets which might help you to land that particular job.

In case you have applied for a job which is different from all your previous jobs and you are changing your field of work too, then you can point out to your interviewer that you are quite a proactive person and fast learner so it shouldn't take you much long to make your mark in this job. You can also provide valid examples where you had made a career shift and have been hired for a position which you didn't have much experience about. Then you can stress on how you were ultimately able to excel in that job.

In all these cases your aim should be to persuade the interviewer that your lack of relevant experience wouldn't be a hindrance in the way of your competent execution of your job responsibilities.

12) Describe your work ethics.

You can deftly answer this question by saying that "work ethics" according to you should describe persons towards his employers. You feel that you are completely committed towards your employers. You always abide by ethical behavior. You can take this opportunity to harp on your ethical traits like punctuality, loyalty and determination.

You can say some thing like this "I always try to show hundred percent commitment towards my job. I try to be punctual in job always and strictly adhere to deadlines. As a loyal employee I am ready to put in that extra effort and persist in a job when difficulties arise and require my efforts. I possess the ability to go the extra mile in order to achieve something which might be beneficial for me as well as the organization."

13) How do you handle an angry customer?

It is quite evident that this question is aimed at checking your public relations and customer handlings skill. If you are being interviewed for a call center or a retail job, this kind of questions can be of uttermost importance. You could say that customer satisfaction is one of the key ways of ensuring good business for an organization. So, we can't afford to let the customers go irate.

You should logically frame your answer in a way which would underscore your dexterity in handling angry customers. You should also emphasize however incensed your customer may be, you cannot afford to behave rudely with a customer. Maintaining your composure and temper is the key tenet of customer handling according to your work profile.

You can add something like this, "The best way to pacify an angry customer is to apologize profusely for whatever grievances have been caused to him. Then I would try to be giving a patient hearing so that I can solve whatever problems he has been having. I would assure him that his problem would be solved in the least possible time and may be try to work a solution which would be feasible for both the customer as well as the organization. Lastly, if the faults have been really from our side, the customer can be given some complimentary service or gifts to ensure that he is further mollified. I would also ensure that all the conversation is conducted in a cordial and polite manner."

14) Can you tell me about a time when you went beyond the call of duty for a customer?

Customer satisfaction is essential for the prosperity of any concern. That's why it's obvious that an interviewer might probe into your customer handling abilities. He would want to ensure whether you would do whatever would be guided by your line of duty or do your possess enough ingenuity, presence of mind and professional zeal to go beyond your line of duty to please your customers.

So, you can expect this sort of questions from your interviewer and you should be well prepared with an answer which would surely woo your interviewer. You can quote an incident which not only would show your customer service skills in the best light but also harp on your pro-activeness and eagerness to please the customers.

You can quote an incident like this "I was working as a customer service executive at a retail outlet. I had taken the order for some Christmas gifts for a lady who was a regular customer of our shop.

However, the stock of those particular gift items got depleted during that festive season and fresh stock also didn't arrive from our main branch in time.

The lady was obviously quite upset to learn that her Christmas shopping plans are turning haywire. She came to my complaint desk quite incensed and demanded a refund. I apologized profusely and went on to give a refund but I also assured her that the stock would be replenished within a day. After my assurance the lady relented and said she was ready to wait for another day and she would come and check after a couple of days.

I realized that we would lose a valuable customer if things went on like this. So, the next day when the fresh stock of those gift items came in I personally took those gift items to her place and also took a complimentary box of chocolates for her after taking my supervisor's permission. This pleased her immensely and she continued her festive shopping with our outlet in the next festive season too." This sort of heartwarming anecdotes would be a sure shot way to win over your interviewer.

15) Do you always make decisions on your own? When do you seek help from others?

You should use this answer to emphasize your independent decision making qualities. You can say that your previous work experiences have taught you to take independent decision and you are quite comfortable taking crucial decisions on your own. You can also provide examples where the success of your team or organization has been ensured due to some key decision that you had taken.

However, it is also important to add that incase you are unsure of the implications or repercussion of your decision you don't hesitate to take the advice or help of your supervisor or co-workers. In other words you should harp that when you think you need a second opinion, you always reach to others for help. This kind of balanced answer would portray your decision making abilities as well as project you as a team player too.

16) How do you handle yourself when you feel everyone is against you?

The interviewer wants to find out how you handle yourself under pressure. Your response should show you are in control of your attitude. He should realize and appreciate the fact that you are a good thinker with good analytical skills and that you don't allow yourself to be a victim.

Thus, you can say, "If I feel I am moving on the right track and if I have management approval to carry on a decision I don't usually waver in my course of action. Some actions might be disapproved by certain co-workers but if it is for the betterment of the company I don't get deterred quite easily." Then you can substantiate your words with a particular challenging situation you might have faced in the course of your career. By asking this sort of question your interview would try to ensure whether you have enough grit and determination to tackle hostile situations.

17) Did you ever fire an associate as a manager?

While answering this question you should simply iterate the truth. If you haven't, say no. If yes, then you need to focus your answer on the true fact that led to such measure. You can say that, "No one wants to let anyone go, however unfortunately at times it is a necessary business decision to keep up the morale and standards high. The key is to do it with respect and dignity. When my company was going through a severe lean phase we had to reduce our work force to survive. As a sales manager even I had to fire some members from my sales team but it was totally a management decision and it was executed with due care and sensitivity."

If you had fired an associate for unethical behavior then you can add that no one should come in the way of fruitful execution of company policies and you could have never condoned such unscrupulous behavior that's why you had to take that decision to fire your colleague.

18) How do you handle difficult people?

This type of questions provides you with the opportunity to put the focus on interpersonal, negotiation and persuasive skills. You can give examples of those previous projects where you have negotiated and mollified difficult clients who were quite hard to please.

You can regale the employer of your success stories where you expertly tackled finicky customers and clients. You can mention that you love difficult people because they stimulate you and help you improve yourself. Try to highlight that handling difficult people is actually a learning process for any professional because trouble shooting abilities is the basic criterion for becoming a good worker.

19) What upsets you or makes you angry?

This is a question which should be answered with care. You can say that you don't condone or relate to people who make the business and people look inefficient and bad. You should try to emphasize that you abhor behaviors like dishonesty, lack of integrity, and waste of resources.

You can say it upsets you to see your colleagues or other people wasting company money or resorting to dishonest means. You can say that since you believe that there is no short cut to success and no replacement of hard work. Seeing people being lazy or indifferent towards their work or resorting to unscrupulous means gets you angry.

However, you should also be quick to emphasize that even if you get irritated and angry with lazy and unscrupulous behavior you never lose your temper enough to resort to any kind of abusive language or violent gestures. You should also emphasize that your displeasure is always bridled by professional decorum.

20) Why are you applying for this job?

Your response should be based on a couple of qualities which you have read in the job description, that are your strengths and apply well to the job. While answering this question, you can say that," I feel that this job would make optimum use of my relevant industry experience, my technical skills as well as my leadership quality". A little bit of flattery about the organization you have applied for won't go amiss but please make sure that you don't over do it.

You can say "Your organization is the market leader in my chosen field and I would like to work with the best people because I feel that would help to bring out the best professional qualities in me." Then you can elaborate on the relevant qualities and positive strengths that you have which might be commensurate for the job.

21) Do you have any regrets?

This question can be answered in multifarious ways. You can simply say "No, I don't have any regrets". However, this would be quite a simplistic way of answering this question and it might not satisfy your interviewer.

While answering this question you should keep your answers limited to the issues of your professional field. However, "Regret" is a very strong word and you should avoid making any confessions to your interviewer about any deep regrets about professional misjudgments you might have made. "You might say that "I don't have any regrets related to my career because I think I have chosen such a field to work on which has huge prospects. I have also had the opportunity to work for some interesting companies and have succeeded in my chosen field."

22) Why did you leave your last job?

Even if this question is apparently quite innocuous, this can prove detrimental towards your job prospects if not handled with care. Many interview candidates make the mistake by stating that they had problems/conflict with managers, supervisors or coworkers and that's why they had to leave that job. Bad mouthing their previous organization and highlighting the lack of opportunity and infrastructure there, actually doesn't help them win any brownie points with the interviewer. Rather it creates a negative impression about them.

So, never speak badly about previous managers and supervisors. The key is to stay positive, regardless of the circumstances. Keep an amicable smile in your face and make sure that your voice sounds positive and enthusiastic and then emphasize the fact that you left for bigger and better opportunities. You can say that you felt there was more room for self growth in your life and thus you left your previous job to move on to greener pastures.

You can say something like this "I had many enjoyable years in my previous job. However, the time is right for new challenge to grow more and have bigger responsibilities." This would be a politically correct way to deal with this tricky question.

23) Do you consider yourself successful?

You should have no hesitation about answering this question and your answer should be a big YES. The interviewer would be watching you minutely to check your confidence level and you should never waver while answering this question. Calmly continue to give a good explanation about some of the goals you have set up and achieved and what new goals you are working on.

You can also substantiate you answer with different successful projects you have conducted or the various academic successes you have had in life. The aim is to make your interviewer understand that you are a confident, goal oriented person and you have a logical way of judging and measuring your success.

24) Are you applying for other jobs?

The best way to answer this is with utmost honesty. However, you should avoid mentioning the names of those organizations. You must also ensure that you don't come across as a desperate candidate who has been applying everywhere. This would cast doubts on your aspirations and competency. So be brief in replying about your job search and also emphasize that your search is very selective.

You should stress that your main focus is on this job and what you offer this organization. You can say "Yes, I have applied for job in few other organizations which are offering the posts of sales managers. However, I am always eager to work for an esteemed organization like yours where I would get the optimum opportunity for growth". Thus, you should state in unequivocal terms that getting this particular job is your first priority.

25) What would your previous direct reports say your strongest points are?

There are several excellent choices you can emphasize on. You can highlight yourself as a- problem solver, passionate person with creative and leadership qualities, possessor of positive attitude, an enthusiastic and goal oriented person, etc. However, be sure to validate your answer with examples, adding possible quotation from one of your co-workers.

You can say, my ex boss "Jill Smith used to say that I am one of the goal oriented sales managers she has ever seen." However, don't fabricate these quotes because they might be cross-checked later. You just need to highlight your true achievements in a positive light.

26) What qualities do you look for in a boss?

The best approach is to answer that you would like your boss to possess those positive qualities which most good managers have. You can say "I would like my boss to be a good mentor and a knowledgeable motivator from whom I can learn the finer nuances of my job and be motivated to excel in it. I would also like him to have a fair sense of judgment and he should also be a good communicator so that no misunderstandings can crop up between us".

You should take this opportunity to emphasize that you are always ready to learn and enhance on your skills from your supervisors and bosses. This would not only underscore the fact that you are a team player but would also give an indication that you know how to respect corporate hierarchy.

27) You will be working with senior/junior staff compared to you, how will you fit in?

You should frame your answer in way which would emphasize that the fact that you are quite at ease working with the junior members of an organization as well the senior management staff. You can also add " I like working an a job which provides me an opportunity to work with different hierarchical level because I feel that diversity creates a good learning environment where one can learn from each other."

You can also justify that interacting with the management staff would help you hone your managerial skills while working with junior employees would help you get a more hands on experience with the production procedure. Your aim should be to impress upon the interviewer your adaptable and malleable nature. He should get that impression that you would be able to adapt yourself to challenging working conditions which involves working with senior officials as well as junior employees.

28) Your resume indicates that your have volunteered at the hospital; tell me about your experience.

If you have done any voluntary work then you should use this to your benefit to impress your prospective employers. Your answer should highlight your humane nature as well as it should underscore what you learnt by interacting with the public. You should not merely provide the skimpy details but rather substantiate your answer with your specific job responsibilities.

You can say, "I was responsible for handling the admission process of the children's ward. I had to deal with a lot of anxious patients. I learned that empathy and cordiality is the best way to handle such delicate situations. I also learnt about the different nitty-gritty's of working as an administrator by working in that hospital."

29) Why did you choose this particular university/college?

By asking this question the interviewer wants to find out about your decision making skills. He wants to know how much well thought out your academic and career decisions were. Your response should show the reasons why you chose that particular institution. Try to elaborate on the points which you considered before joining that particular university or college.

If you were wooed by the program they offered then dwell on these particular points. You can also say that your decision was based on research and point out what other school or colleges you considered of enrolling before you selected that particular college. However, be sure not to give any flippant answers like "My College was in the locality that we resided, and was easier to commute". This kind of apathetic attitude would surely act against you.

30) Were you ever fired or terminated?

This is a very difficult question to answer, especially if you left under bad circumstances. The key is not to dwell on the past and don't let bitterness come out. Your answer should be very short and quickly change the topic if you can. You can respond with statements like, "My position was outsourced," or "The plant closed down," or "The Company downsized," or "It was a mutual agreement due to lack of work." Just remember keeping your answers succinct and short is the key to answer this question.

However, please don't lie while answering this question and try to camouflage your termination. They would surely find out about the reasons behind your leaving the last job when they do a background check. So, you should be as much honest as possible. Just don't go on elaborating the reasons or let any acrimony about your erstwhile boss or your previous organization creep into your voice while you answer this question.

Thus, the next time you go for an interview do ensure that you have got your listening cap on and try your level best to get a true understanding of what the interview is looking for with each question. You should formulate your answers accordingly to stress the fact that you have got the necessary skills for the job.

CHAPTER 10

HOW TO SURVIVE YOUR FIRST 90 DAYS IN A JOB

"The road to excellence is always under construction." ~ Ramzi Karim

Congratulation you got the job!!

After a tedious application procedure and grueling rounds of interview you have finally landed your dream job. However, this is not simply the beginning of a dream run. Now, as a new employee of the organization it remains up to you to shine and rise to the occasion.

People take up a job for various reasons. It helps people to make a decent living, satisfy their dreams and desires, grow personally, professionally, put their knowledge to work and contribute to the society. Thus, working should not be only about getting just a pay check. Confucius quite aptly said *"**Choose a job you love, and you will never have to work a day in your life.**"* If you are able to successfully handle your new job and are showered with appreciation then you would be more willing to take on the long hours and the other job related worries that tag along with that job. That is why it is quintessential to start working to making a success out of your new job from the very beginning.

It is understandable to be nervous, excited, and anxious at the same time when you join a new organization. You should make no mistake in realizing that all the eyes will be on the new kid on the block. Other staff members will watch every move you make regardless of the designation you have joined in. All your co-workers are going to develop their perception of you and without you realizing, you will be partly responsible for the kind of perception they will shape about you.

Thus, is important to realize that every action you take will bring a reaction among the team. Therefore starting on the right foot from day one is very critical. One single faux pas that you make during your first 90 days in your job might irrefutably tarnish your image as a competent worker. Whether you are just a junior executive or the new finance manager of the company, people will be equally critical and judgmental about your work if you are unable to deliver what you had promised during your interview.

The first 90 days also referred to as probationary period. This period allows you to evaluate your employer and for the employer to evaluate you so that if either party are unhappy the employment can be terminated quickly. Even though there is no hard and fast rules about probationary periods but usually employers tend to treat probationers differently than regular employees. The employers are often more keen on checking out the mettle of the probationers on various aspects of the job. Employers often need to ensure that the decision they had taken by employing you was a correct one. It's you who has to prove your merit as a valuable asset to the company.

In this chapter we will focus on some key elements that will ensure your success at work place in the first ninety days in particular and afterwards in general.   Some of the archetypal qualities which are discussed below are the common denominators for success in a job. The exemplary qualities that you need to imbibe in order to achieve success in your new job are:

- **Positive Mental Attitude**

- **Goal Setting Capabilities**

- **Observation Power**

- **Adaptability**

- **Ability to take Initiative**

- **Team Spirit**

- **Integrity and Strength of Character**

- **Leadership Qualities**

Positive Mental Attitude

> *"Big jobs usually go to men who show the ability to outgrow smaller jobs"*—Theodore Roosevelt.

A positive frame of mind is one of the key qualities to have to be successful in life and work. Your positive attitude to life helps people understand about your mental strength and appreciate your outlook towards work and life. Mastering a positive mental attitude will allow you to make a difference at your work environment. It is your positive attitude and minuscule behavioral pattern which might make a difference in people's life and may change the perception of your co-workers about you.

Don't Act in a Grumpy Manner

If you allow yourself to grumble about your new work environment or complain even a little about the facilities and environment in your current job people will quick to brand you as pessimistic and negative person.

The co-workers might say "I don't like his attitude", 'He is grumpy all the time", "He never smiles", "He is so negative" and "He never says please and thank you". These are all mental pictures which people develop of a person very quickly at work place. This is especially the case if the person took a job which someone else from inside the company has applied for. The inherent resentment that a new joiner faces quickly fuels the rumors about his negative attitude and grumpy behavior.

To avoid falling in this trap you need to make sure that you come across   positive and enthusiastic person from the first day of your job. This is easier said than done, especially if you face continuous setbacks in your new job. However, you must not let your frustration and irritation with your co-workers or the company policies have a visible impact on your behavior and demeanor. You should avoid making derogatory comments about your company at any cost. Even if the food available in your company cafeteria tastes like saw dust don't keep on being irritable about it when you are out on a lunch break with your colleagues.

Be Positive and Cordial

Try to instill a bright and sunny persona and avoid appearing peevish. When some one puts forward any idea in a group meeting be sure not to brush it off tetchily. Even if you can't agree to the idea put forward by the person be sure to appreciate the new idea and then put your own arguments against it. It is always a great idea to make people feel important and appreciating people would always earn you some brownie points with them. This however doesn't mean that you have to be obsequious but it simply means that some positive gestures and approving words for your colleagues always goes an extra mile to establish you as a cordial and positive person.

Another essential part of having a positive attitude in work is to appreciate constructive criticism. You should never let criticism bog you down and affect your performance. You should have a profound faith in your capabilities and you should allow criticism to egg you on towards better performance rather than make you depressed.

There will be fake perfectionists in every office who would find flaws in every project delivered or every job done by you. However, you should simply shift through the barrage of criticism and take those constructive suggestions which might help you in future.

Goal setting Capabilities

The Oxford Dictionary defines the word 'goal' in the following way: 'A goal is a point marking end of a race; an object of effort or ambition'. In other words a goal is an end result that you want or choose to work toward for your personal development. The true character of a man is identified by the goals or ambitions in life that he nurtures.

Job related goals or ambitions are definitely an important part of the overall life goals of a man. This is especially true for a new job where the environment is new and you have a lot to prove. Starting new with a new job, whether you are experienced at it or not, is about managing expectations. As a matter of fact, nothing makes you manage job expectations better than setting correct job oriented goals. Goals get you organized, make you focused and give you a sense of accomplishment.

Short Term and Long Term Goals

To start effectively in setting goals in your new work place begin with making sure that you have a copy of the job description with you. Perusing the job description minutely would help you in two ways. Firstly, it would ensure that you have a complete understanding of what is expected of you and what goals and objectives you need to set to be successful in short term as well as on long term basis.

Secondly, if you are aware of the different nuances of the job description, it would help you to reach out for common goals which would be commensurate with the expectations that your reporting head might have from you. The goals you set for yourself should never clash with company policies or the expectations of your superiors from you. This might lead to friction in your work life and show you as an irreverent subordinate.

Henry Ford once said ***"Nothing is particularly hard if you divide it into small jobs."*** So, the goals set for in your job should clearly identify what you want to achieve in your job and how you plan to achieve it. You should set short term as well as long term goals to ensure all round success.

For example, you have joined as a sales manager of a company. If your company has been going through a lean phase, then your long term goal would obviously be to augment the drooping sales figures of your company. It remains up to you to formulate a clear cut short term goal to achieve your long term goal. You can device a new training program for your sales team and print a new sales manual to ensure that the sales figures get boosted soon.

Realistic Goals

Another important thing that you should keep in mind while setting up goals in your new job is that your goals should always be realistic and achievable. It's a great thing to dream big but your goals should never be so huge that you fail to achieve them in the end. You should make an objective judgment whether your goals are accessible within the time frame you have set for yourself.

For example, if you have joined as the CEO of a company which is running on heavy losses and you set the goal to establish your organization as one of the top ten companies in your field within six months, then that might be an unrealistic goal given the time frame. Unrealistic goals might not materialize leading to disillusionment and depression. These may be great as dreams but goals in life need to be based more on realistic facts. If you keep these criteria in mind while you set up your goals as a new employee, then you will give yourself the best probable chance of achieving the things you want.

Observation Power

Keen observation power is a quintessential quality for any new employee. If you need to blend in positively with your company's work environment and prove yourself as an excellent worker then you need to observe and internalize the work related measures and decision making procedures that are prevalent in your company. It's not bad to come up with new and ingenious ideas but where many new joiners err, in that they try to bring and make too many changes too soon, it often might not be well appreciated.

Don't Make Drastic Changes within a Short Time

When starting in a new job, many employees make the mistake of making changes without asking anybody. To avoid this major pitfall you must improve your observational skills. You need to observe the culture of the company and be vigilant about the spoken and unspoken accepted behaviors. You should always be on your toes lest you put your wrong foot forward and make a fool of yourself.

The other employees will be observing minutely and the moment they catch you doing wrong things, they might make a big story out of your faux pas. You would surely not want the stories of your inadvertent mistake doing the rounds of the office grape vine. So, it is imperative to enhance your observational power and adapt with the company environment as quickly as possible.

Joining a new job is always an awkward phase but you shouldn't be hasty in judging the company or your coworkers and take decisions for drastic change without consulting your colleagues. To help you improve your observational skills you need to be a good friend of the two "Ws". You need to be aware of "What" is going on in your new organization and seek out "Why" those decisions are being implemented.

Let me give you a true life example with an incident which happened to me once. I was given a new unit to manage in an organization which I had just joined. I came to the place and observed many processes which were not up to the mark and obviously didn't find my approval. As a result, I immediately started changing things around without consulting my co-workers.

Yes, you guessed it, right a barrage of complaints started to fly all over the places immediately after the changes desired by me were put to effect. My decision and changes met with a lot of resentment from other employees of the unit. My co workers and subordinates started saying things like "Who does he think he is?", "If not broken don't fix it", "We like things the way they are". Quite naturally, soon I was called up by my supervisor who sat down with me and gave me a sage lesson which I never forgot. He gave the valuable lesson that before you embark on any venture to change any existing procedure, you should first find out **"WHAT** they do?" then "Find out WHY they do it?"

Observe and Find out about the Existing Procedures

Without gleaning detailed information about any existing rule or procedure in your organization you should not hastily start making key changes. After finding out how things work out if you still have any resourceful idea about how to make things work better then discuss it with your team mates and reporting heads. The key is to come to a solution together which is acceptable to every one. I found out that this line of thinking always works like magic in making your new job environment more conducive and friendly.

Einstein had once said *"Curiosity is more important than knowledge"*.

When you join a new organization try take the help of the people who have been in the organization for a long time and learn from them. You should never aim to metamorphose things in your company quickly. Try to find out about the existing options, resources and procedures which are already there in that particular organization. Aim to formulate new rules and formats which would be commensurate with the existing options.

If you are really enthusiastic about any program or project which was hugely successful in your previous company then you should try to make an objective judgment on whether that can be successful in your current organization too. Even after a long deliberation, if you feel that the same policy should work out fine there too, then you should suggest the idea as if it's your own.

Don't try to put up comparisons with your old organization saying "We tried this in my previous company". You should rather try to test the waters by saying, "What if we try this out?" or "What do you think of this idea?" This would be a much more positive approach to put forward your ideas and views without sounding too overbearing or supercilious.

Adaptability

Every organization is unique and each organization has its unique needs and specific work culture and work procedures. Even such small things such as communication method, common attitudes, and the daily goals of the organization are significant tell-tale signs of the corporate culture of an organization. You'll need to adapt your work approach to fit the work program of your boss, reporting head, and coworkers. So, you should be patient enough to take the time to learn what works for that organization and what doesn't by merely being friendly with an old hand or by simply asking your supervisor.

Adapting To a New Environment

Getting a job also introduces a new environment to individuals and this new environment brings major changes with it. To be successful in any new job you must be able to manage this change and adjust to the new environment. The first 90 days in any job is a time for learning adaptations and adjustments. You need to have the determination, grit and strength of character to tide you through the rough spots you might face during this period and craft a strong foundation for your future with the company.

You should never start panicking from the very beginning. To adjust properly in a new work environment you need to see change not as a fearsome proposition, but rather as a challenge. You have to act with patience and give yourself time to acclimatize with the new job environment, new co-workers and novel work processes. The key of surviving successfully in a new job is to boldly cope with the change even when you are besieged with unexpected responsibilities.

If you are a dedicated observer and a keen learner then you would soon find out about each and every facet of your organization. This would help you to come up with ideas and plans which would be appropriate with the work culture of that organization. Don't try to impose your own stringent ideas which are not approved by others, this would only hinder you from adapting yourself in your current work place.

Don't Criticize

Making snide remarks about your company and comparing it with your previous organization would be like committing a professional hara-kiri. You should never make condescending remarks like "This did not work in my previous company". This would simply raise the hackles of your co-workers and make you feel like an outsider.

Thus, you should always try to blend with you co-workers and the work culture of that organization as smoothly as possible. It won't help your performance if you always stick out like a sore thumb in your team or in your office. So, the adaptability is a great quality which you need to imbibe in yourself, if you want to taste the sweet fruits of success in your new job.

Ability to take Initiatives

Elbert Hubbard the famous American writer and editor once commented" ***Initiative is doing the right thing without being told***". This comment is quite vital in the perspective of successful execution of new job responsibilities. Ability to take initiative is always appreciated in a new employee. If you want to reach the zenith of success in your new job then you should always try to become pro-active in what you do. However, in order to be good at taking initiatives you should be quick witted, hardworking and logical. If you want to take responsibilities proactively you need to act, think and plan ahead.

Start Your Initiatives from the Day you Join

Your efforts at taking initiative starts from the day you join. When you join an organization, you have to quickly ensure that your work space is all set up and that you have the equipments and computer passwords that require doing your job. You shouldn't passively wait for others to make these arrangements for you. It's true that a good employer usually has all these basic facilities set up even before you join your work but sometimes the case is a little different. In certain cases employers deliberately leave things half done so that they can test your initiative taking abilities.

So, when you join your work and can't find your computer password or basic equipments, things might seem too disorganized or you might brand your new employer as downright rude; but don't jump to conclusions. This might be their way of checking how adjusting you are and how quickly you can take initiatives and set up whatever you require for your work.

Your employers would keenly observe whether you sit passively remain perched on your seat waiting for someone to provide you those equipments and passwords or you proactively seek some one from the systems department and procure the new password for your computer yourself. They would also keep an eye on your temperament to see whether you are relaxed and accommodating about the extra effort you had to put in or you threw a fit because your work space was not all set up when you joined work.

Taking initiative sometimes might entail going out of your way to help out the organization. If you really want to take initiatives and want to establish yourself as a proactive worker then you should not always confine yourself within your charted job responsibilities and departmental duties. Your approach towards your work should always be enthusiastic and wholehearted.

Don't be Indifferent

You should never act in an indifferent manner and comment "This is not my responsibility", or "There is some one else to do this job". This would definitely create a negative impression in the minds of your new employers. They might stamp you as an escapist and think that you lack the passion and zing to prove a valuable asset for the organization. If someone seeks your help regarding some organizational issues and you brush him off saying "I don't want to get involved", then you would simply lose a golden opportunity to prove your mettle as a superior organizer and a keen worker.

Try to Be Pro-Active

You can take initiative in any area of your work place which might need improvement. However, you should be methodical in your efforts. Trying to figure out ways to help your boss is one of the primary initiatives you need to take. When you are able to provide immense support to your superiors by being their right arm, then you become an indispensable asset for the organization. This subsequently would aid you to stand out in a crowd of workers and get noticed and appreciated soon. So, proper initiatives should be the stepping stone of your success in a new organization.

To further help you with improving your initiative skills, you should keep the following principles in mind:

- **Understand your job responsibilities**
- **Think how you can perform your job more efficiently**
- **Think of problems even before they arise**
- **Handle your priorities effectively**

- **Be innovative**

- **Don't be bull-headed**

Team Spirit

Every organization wants its employees to be team players to ensure greater productivity for an organization. To be successful in your new job you must actively participate and engage yourself with the team you are joining. Your job will be to make everyone of your team feel comfortable working with you, and to work together to make your team a winning team. No body appreciates a loner and if you want to be successful at your job, then you have to work as a team player.

As a team player you must always underscore your positive attitude and team spirit. Your willingness to strive for the overall success of your team should come across to your co-workers. You have to be able to work together towards a common goal or vision. To be a good team player you must be a humble student and learn from everyone, more importantly from your mistakes. You have to come out playing hard with same grit and determination in every shift and show as the great hockey maestro Wayne Gretzky once said **"You are only as good as your last shift"**.

Encourage all Team Members

You should never get involved in unhealthy competition with other team members. Your aim should be to compete with your self and come up with better performance, which would in turn encourage and challenge other team members to do their duties with perfection. You have to excel in each and every performance. You should always ensure that each and every member of your team should have a clear cut function within the team. Allocating definite job goals for every member of the team would reduce the chances of having ego clashes and miscommunication. So, as a team player your aim should be to achieve a fine balance and a winning partnership with each and every member of your team.

Resolve Conflicts Cordially

Chances are that despite all these there might be some squabble between you and other team members. Resolving conflicts in an amicable manner is the intrinsic characteristic of a great team player. You should never arrogantly stick to your own view rather you should be malleable enough for members to see things from the view point of other team members. Otherwise it would be quite hard for your team to stick together and work effortlessly. Your team spirit would ultimately benefit you in the end because by working as a cohesive team you can achieve the impossible. Team work would allow you to surpass such mountains which you yourselves could have never done.

Get Proper Feedback

An enormous part of integrating yourself into a new job is getting to know your colleagues and supervisors who would also be your team members. This process of knowing your team members also encompasses the knowledge of what your team members think about your performance and work. You should be quite aware from the beginning what the team members think about the quality of work.

Getting detailed feed back from your team members would serve a dual purpose. This would help you to customize your performance as per the needs of the team and come up with a more brilliant feat. On the other hand it would also help people know how much you appreciate their views and feedbacks.

Integrity and Strength of Character

Malcolm Forbes once commented, *"**Diamonds are nothing but chunks of coal that stuck to their jobs**".* A new job is the right place to prove your mettle and show your strength of character as well as integrity. You must have sold yourself well during the interview and that is why you landed the coveted job bypassing other candidates. However, after you have started working for an organization, the true test of your skills starts. The employers also get a chance to test whether you are merely filled with sound and fury or whether you can deliver what you promise.

Don't Promise What you Can't Deliver

Thus, your strength of character, your honesty and integrity comes into play from the rounds of interview that you face and from the time even before you are selected for a particular job. Your are definitely going to trip and falter when you join a new job, if you had promised something you are incapable of or emphasized a skill set which you don't posses. So, it is imperative that during your interview as well as during the first few days of your job, you don't get too overzealous about selling your self and sing paeans of your past achievements which actually never happened. There is nothing wrong presenting yourself in a good light, but it is always recommended that you stick to the facts.

Take People's Help to Know Things Better

There is nothing wrong in seeking people's help if you don't know about something. You are not expected to be a know-it-all. If you can't understand a process of work you can always walk up to an experienced person and ask for directions. This would not disgrace you but would rather emphasize your willingness to learn. So, when you are a new employee in your enthusiasm to prove yourself as a worthy asset don't lose your integrity and straightforward character.

Accept your Errors

Integrity defines who you are, what your values are and how you keep your promise. An employee of true character and integrity is expected to take the responsibility of actions and clarify himself when he does something which is wrong or isn't approved of. Thus, during the few weeks of your job even if you put a wrong foot forward or make an error inadvertently, then you should come up with proper explanation of the cause of your error in judgment. However, it remains up to you to avoid such mistakes at all cost.

There is nothing wrong in making mistakes while doing your job. You are not expected to be infallible even though perfection is always appreciated. However, if you falter in an area which might cast aspirations on your honesty and integrity, it might cost you dearly. If you make some insalubrious or shady choices in your new job, then you have to pay an immense price for your lack of honesty and veracity.

Never Indulge in Immoral Practices

Thus, never try to indulge in any unscrupulous practice in your job. Even if you have unwittingly made some errors which might be criticized, come forward with it and don't try to cover that up because that would further aggravate the situation and cast aspirations about your integrity. The biggest price that you have to pay would be your loss of respect. If they perceive you as untruthful and unfair, they would simply lose the respect that they have for you and your credentials.

Loss of respect is a critical situation for a new employee because earning back people's respect is quite hard. Earning respect involves changing people's perception about you and that might take a long time. For example, you work in the accounts department and there have been some unsuspecting errors in the balance sheet on your part. In such a situation you should immediately bring that to the notice of the management. If you try to cover that up, they might later doubt your honesty and think that you were trying to siphon money from the company. This would be a grave situation because not only disciplinary measures can be taken against you, but your image as an honest worker would also get besmeared.

Benjamin Franklin had once aptly said, **"Success has ruined many a man"**. Many people fail the integrity test when temptation presents it self. You must know your strengths and weaknesses and your vulnerability. So, do the right thing and don't let your ambition and quest for successes tempt you. Success can be a heady enticement and causes the downfall of many men of character. You should always keep in mind there is no short cut to success.

Integrity at work also involves not turning a blind eye to what others do. If you find a big integrity breach from coworkers, you must either confront it your self or report it to proper people. If you want to take a short route to success and succumb to the temptation of unscrupulous means and unethical colleagues, that would merely tarnish your image and bring an unexpected end to your bright career with the organization.

Leadership Qualities

According to Edwin H. Friedman *"Leadership can be thought of as a capacity to define oneself to others in a way that clarifies and expands a vision of the future"*.

Leadership quality is a quality which is always commended and appreciated in a new employee. If you are able to display leadership qualities in your new job then you stand out from the crowd and garner the respect from your superiors and co-workers. Your employers would value you more for your leadership qualities because this would mean that you have the potential to climb up the corporate ladder quite quickly and lead the company in times of need.

Lead By Example

If you want to imbibe leadership qualities in yourself then you must lead by example and encourage your team members to follow your exemplary work efficiency. However, in order to achieve this goal you have to strive hard to ensure that your own performance is of highest echelon. In other words as a team leader you need to inculcate in yourself such fine qualities which you expect from your team members.

For example, if you want your subordinates and co-workers to be punctual you should always arrive in office on time. If you are always late for meetings or are always dashing for your office room after your scheduled arrival time, then you can't dictate your team members to be punctual and time bound. If needs be, as a team leader you should be the first to arrive and the last one to leave the office. This grueling schedule might be a little hard to follow but this would earn you respect from your team members who would appreciate you for the respect you are putting in. So, as a leader you should always have a flexible schedule to accommodate the different needs of your team.

Don't be Overbearing or Highhanded

You should teach others how to solve problems and troubleshoot efficiently. Your team members should look unto you for advice and guidance. Thus, as a true leader you should be capable of being a positive influence on your workforce, and thus effectively maintain team unity. However, you should make sure that as a leader you are never overbearing and high handed. You should have enough modesty to take the help of your team leaders when you need it.

There is no thumb rule that a leader has to be flawless. You should be unpretentious enough to accept feed back and constructive criticism positively. Don't give irrelevant and false excuses to cover up your mistakes or error or judgment because that would only earn you the disrespect and ire of your colleagues. If you commit mistakes while leading your team, then accept your error of judgment with humility, and try to learn from your mistakes. In fact, a good sense of humor would help you in this regard. If you have an alteration with some body or face criticism from someone this would help you to lighten the situation and prevent things from getting too uncomfortable and tense.

However, you should take care that you do not repeat your mistakes time and again. Learning from mistakes is the key quality of a good leader. In order to avoid making mistakes in future you should broaden your horizon and try to glean information about a wide array of topics related to the field of your work. As they say "knowledge is power" and with enough know-how in your kitty, you would soon shine in meeting and come up with ingenious ideas. All you need is unwavering confidence in your abilities to lead your team. In other words, if you put your mind to it you can soon bedazzle your employers with your fine performance and leadership qualities.

If these guide lines are implemented successfully then they would definitely help your cause in becoming a leader.

Summing up...

I guarantee that if you can follow and implement the principles which are elucidated in this chapter, you will pass the your first ninety days in your job with flying colors. Ingraining these quintessential qualities of a good employee would help you to achieve success in your job beyond your probationary period. As Marva Collins aptly said "Success doesn't come to you... you go to it."

Just keep these key things in mind and everything will pass smoothly. Imbibing the aforementioned traits in yourself would help your productivity. A little change in your attitude would ensure complete satisfaction to your self, your boss as well as your team members.

CHAPTER 11

ADVICE TO PARENTS

"Your children need your presence more than your presents." ~Jesse Jackson

The bond between a child and his parents is perhaps the tenderest and the strongest bond in the world. Your children not only depend on you for their basic needs but they look up to them also. Parents are parenting educators rather than simply the mother and father of the children. Thus, as parents it is your duty to support, nurture and encourage the children to rise up and build their careers.

In recent years, I have interviewed a large number of teenagers for entry level jobs. Most of these jobs were part-time jobs or summer jobs but a few of them were also full time jobs. The age of students applying for these jobs ranged from fifteen year olds, who were starting their first year of high school, to older students, who were already attending university or college for a few years. Over the years I have seen how parents have helped or hindered their kids' ability to get entry level jobs. I have minutely noticed the crucial impact the parents have on the careers of these young adolescents.

Why do Adolescents start working early now?

In these tough economic times getting jobs has become much harder, due to the large number of people applying for work. The current economic recession has cast a pall of gloom over the world economy and pay cuts and job loss has become a norm of the day. Students are often forced to seek jobs early into their career due to various reasons.

Many students are forced to work very early in their life due to their parent's job loss and pay cuts. Recession has brought with it the menace of inflation and considerable increase in the cost of living. This hefty rise in the cost of living and dwindling of disposable income of their guardians and parents often put additional pressure on high school, college and university students to start working early.

All these economic factors make it imperative for students to prepare for the job search well in advance. The changes in the current economic conditions and technological advancements have in turn metamorphosed the employment markets dramatically. Plum jobs are not as easy to find as it was earlier. However, the buoyant part of this gloomy scenario is that the skills and qualities necessary for success in the interview as well as the work place remains the same. The fact remains that as a parent you can significantly contribute to map out the career choices as well as ensure the successes of your children. It greatly depends on you to extend a helping hand to your teenager to find his first job.

How can you help?

In this chapter we are going to talk about how as parents you can help your teenager to get the first taste of the real world when it comes to employment. We would elucidate to you the ways in which you can support them on their quest for a successful career. The wrong career notions of the parents have often marred the efforts of a bright candidate while proper encouragement from the parents have helped an average candidate to land a coveted job with ease.

Thus, before you venture out to help your teenager kids to find their first jobs you should keep certain key things in mind. You should be organized and methodical in your attempt to help them make the right choices and guide then to augment their skills and credentials. The "P.E.A.C.E" concept which we will talk about in this chapter should give you excellent advice on how to help your inexperienced teenager on their mission to carve out a bright career and seek a good job.

P.E.A.C. E is the acronym for

- **Prepare**
- **Encourage**
- **Advice**
- **Challenge**
- **Evaluate**

Now, let's go and find out in detail about each of these major criterions which would be like a beacon of light in your quest to fruitfully help your teenager children to shape up their career.

Prepare

Like any other venture in life when your child embarks on a journey to shape up his career it requires a lot of preparations. If you want your offspring to succeed in his dream career then you should prepare and equip him for it in all possible ways. Some of the key ways in which you can boost up the job prospects of your progeny are enlisted below.

Help him to create a Perfect Resume

One of the key ingredients for a successful job search is a perfect resume. The resumes are used by personnel managers to weed out the potential candidates. Thus, if you want your teenage children to be interviewed by the potential employers then help him to create a perfect resume. A concise yet powerful resume would convince the prospective employers about the key qualities of your youngster. You can also help him to create multiple versions of the resume and cover letter tailored for individual jobs. This would help them to identify their key strengths and major weaknesses.

However, before you embark on creating a good resume along with your kid you should find out the basics of writing a great resume. Gleaning information about which format should be ideal for your teenager child who is still student is also important. A functional resume is ideal for students and fresheners who have too little professional experience. Thus, you can make optimum use of a functional resume to highlight the academic and other extra-curricular experiences of your child and downplay the lack of relevant industry experience. This would highlight the functional skills that life has taught him.

A first-rate resume will allow the prospective employers to locate all relevant information about your kid such as his educational qualifications, voluntary and social service experiences etc without any trouble. It is always expected that a resume be grammatically error-free and written in impeccable language. Creating a resume which contains spelling errors and sloppy language would be like committing a professional hara-kiri. Thus, you should review your child's resume for proper structure, content, grammar and spelling errors.

Conduct Mock Interviews

Apart from creating a resume you should also help your child to prepare for interview. The ideal way to do this is to conduct mock interviews. If your teenager is quite shy then chances are that he might be dumbstruck in front of the interviewers. By conducting mock interviews not only can you help him practice his interview answers but you can also aid him to get rid of his fear of public speaking. Try to role play as the interviewer and assess the interview answers with true objectivity. This would help you to fine tune his answers and enhance on his interview performance.

Job Shadowing or Practical Exposure to a Work Environment

Reading about occupations is quite an easy task but gleaning information about an occupation and getting a first hand feel about it are two different ball game altogether. A hands-on experience always works well with teenagers because it provides them with a first hand feel about work life. This is called job shadowing. Thus, the best way you can prepare your children for their future careers is by exposing them to a real-life work environment.

For the aforementioned purpose you can take him to your work place one day and show him around the various departments and work processes. You should let him observe how office protocols are maintained and how things get done on time. You can also introduce him to your colleagues who might provide him with further details about different nuances of your work. This would help your child to form a concrete idea about work ethics, work culture and different types of interpersonal interaction that goes on in an office. It would also help him to comprehend how official hierarchy is maintained and respected.

Let him Know in Details about your Own Career

Josh Billings once aptly commented "**To bring up a child in the way he should go, travel that way yourself once in a while.**"

You can encourage your teenage sons or daughters to be interested in a professional life by talking about how your own career had developed in the past. It would be great fun to tenderly reminisce about your own trials and tribulations with your career and it will definitely aid you better to understand what problems your son might be facing. If you chart out the events and people that have affected your career it would not only make it quite easy for you to appreciate the various influences that are shaping his unique journey towards achieving a successful career but it would also help him know more about the facts of life and the problems that he might face.

Encourage

Parents need to encourage their teenage children to be themselves. Often parents get too overzealous about carving out a successful career for their adolescent children and in the process they stifle the individuality and talent that their children might possess. You should always help your children find out their calling and their own talents while providing guidance from the back ground. However, many parents forget where to draw the line in their eagerness to help their children with their careers and as a result they damage their self esteem rather than helping them out.

As an interviewer I have had many such instances in my life. Let me provide you with some real life examples which would help you to avoid making such mistakes in your own life. I have noticed it quite a lot of time that many young candidates come to apply for a job with their parents. There is nothing wrong in it. However, in certain cases the parents become too effusive in talking about their children.

They usually come up with lines like this "My son/daughter would really like working here. He is an efficient child too. Could you please allot him an interview date?" In other cases, the parents start enquiring in details about hours of operation, work environment and payments etc. They also hand in the resume on behalf of their children.

Usually, all this happens while the kids stand on the background keeping mum. This is a situation which is quite damaging for the job prospects of the candidate. If you think from the interviewer's point of view you would understand how detrimental the situation is for the job success of the kid. In such a situation it is quite natural for an interviewer to think of the following things about the candidate:

- **The candidate lacks confidence**

- **He cannot communicate effectively**

- **He is afraid of public speaking**

- **He is very timid**

- **He lacks social and interpersonal skills**

It is quite obvious that these types of candidates are least likely to make it to the interview rooms. So, you should never try to mollycoddle your children in such a manner which infact becomes harmful for his career. Let him handle job applications and interviews in a confident manner

Take Help of Various Career Services

You can encourage him to take part in volunteer work for different social service organization or engage him in internship with different firms. You can also coax him to take help of the various career services office which are available in all schools, colleges and universities. The student mentors and career counselors available through these career service and career placement centers of different schools and colleges can help your child in multiple ways.

These student mentors and career counselors would evaluate the interests, personality and skill-set of your kid. As per their evaluation, they would ask your kid to survey different recommended career options. These career service offices can also provide valuable information to the students about resume writing, interview preparation and effective way to job search. A career counselor would also provide your youngster specialized assistance to help his transition from student to professional life.

Not only schools and colleges many local communities often have career clubs to help teenage children find their ideal vocation. These career clubs often hold seminars where presenters come to tell club members about their jobs. Field trips are also helpful for members to visit different work sites. You can also enroll your child in such career clubs to find his footing in his desired career.

Encourage your child to Network

Incidentally, all the jobs that are advertised in the newspaper only form a small portion of the jobs that are available in the market. Infact, survey proves that 75% of the available jobs are not advertised. Employers often try to find prospective employees through personal references or they simply can't afford the cost of advertisements. This is especially true for low-key or junior level jobs in which a teenager or student can apply for. That is why it is imperative for your child to keep his eyes and ears open if he wants to seriously search for a job.

You should also encourage your youngster to network with his friends, teachers, community leader, and student mentors and try to find out maximum job related information. It might so happen that a friend who has applied for a job might inform him about it. If he keeps his teachers and student mentors updated about his job quest they might also refer him to some prospective employers. Thus, opportunities might arrive from any form. However, you must not always breathe down his neck every day asking him how his job search is going on. This would make him all the more uncomfortable. You just need to make sure that he is in touch with the right people who can help him to find a job.

Advice

The famous poet Oscar Wilde once commented **"The only thing to do with good advice is to pass it on. It is never of any use to oneself"**. I know it is hard at times to advise and coach teenagers. Teenagers often think they have enough know how to guide their lives in the right track and nurture the opinion that are infallible. In certain cases teenagers are too attached to his or her peer group and trust their friend's opinion more than their parents or guardians.

Don't Preach while giving Advice

All these factors often complicate the situation for the parents and make the task of giving advice to teenagers really an arduous one. Regardless of this fact as parents you must go on to advice him so that he doesn't take such decisions which he might come to rue in future. As teenagers are often quite reluctant to receive advice and coaching from their parents, you have to be quite tactful while you do so. If you use a supercilious tone and haughty manner while advising your children they would simply shut you out.

You need to teach your young charges proper social responsibilities as well as make them aware of the problems they might encounter while they try to build up their career. However, all these must not be done in preachy tone; rather your tone should be friendly and cordial so that your teenager doesn't get overwhelmed or bored.

Try to give Advice as a Friend

If you go on to give a droning lecture to your adolescent son about the trials and tribulations he might face in life and how to shape up his career just the way you did, he would simply feel overwhelmed and irritated. The key is to find the right time and the right way to provide your advice and coaching. In order to ensure the optimum career development of your adolescent children it is imperative not to preach them but rather be friendly with them. So the ideal quality of getting your advice heeded by your children is friendship.

Encourage him to participate in creative activities and spend some quality time with him. While doing so you can also casually broach the topic of his career plans and then elaborate on it. For example, you two can go to a movie together. Later on, after returning from the movie, may be during a meal, you can start discussing about the different characters of that movie and their work life and life roles.

Then you can quietly broach the topic of the work life of different people and what implications they might have on lifestyle choices. So, the bottom line is that you have to be friendly and tactful when you advice your child about his career choices.

Advice him on the Financial Aspects of Life

Your responsibilities as parents are endless. You must elaborate on the fact that there is no short cut to success. If he has already got a part time job which provides him some amount of financial independence then he must be quite buoyed by it. It is up to you to remind him of his long term goal of completing his college education and finding a job which would be appropriate for his academic credentials and inner potentials.

You must advice him on how to save his hard earned money for his college fund or future business plans. This might raise his hackles and he might brand this as an effort to curb his independence, but you have to reason with him without losing your temper. Often his friends might encourage him to splurge his money but you should be the one to offer advice about having a spendthrift nature and help him consolidate his funds for future use like enrolling into a vocational course, or college fees.

However, you have to practice what you preach. If you are always ranting and raving about his over-spending habits, then you must not also over indulge yourself in extravagant things.

Don't Compare and Criticize while Advising

You have the desire to see your children to be successful in life. You expect to see them in satisfying careers with immense potential for growth. The very thought of seeing your children getting stuck in menial and dead-end jobs is quite depressing for you. However, in your enthusiasm to help your child you must not hamper his self esteem.

You should be careful about not wounding his morale by comparing him with his more successful peers and providing real life instances of successful careers to him. Each adolescent is special and you need to accept him as he is. You have to appreciate his positive qualities and then advice him on how he can augment his skills and potential and reach the zenith of success.

If he is keen on choosing a particular career path then don't just refute him in an overbearing manner. You can just put forward your own logic and recommend other career choices. The last thing you should do is to tell him that he doesn't have enough abilities to succeed in the career of his choice. This would reduce his self esteem and thus the very purpose of your well meaning advice would be undermined.

So, try not to directly discourage your child from a particular career even if you think it is wrong for him. All you can do is to put forward some other enticing career choices and encourage him to decide on his own.

Keep yourself Updated on the Recent Career Options

Thus, the way to put forward your advice is of quintessential importance. They sometimes even believe that as parents you are out of touch with the current trend and the advice you are giving are out of date. To prove him wrong in these notions you have to keep yourself updated about the latest career choices and the professional courses available so that you can prove him that your advice would be of immense help to him. You can take the help of internet to search for the career options for your children. You can also garner information about the vocational course that might help your child to grab that prize job which he dreams of getting.

Advice him to Know more about Current Affairs

If your teenager child is looking for a job then you can advice him to glance through the newspaper headlines every day and keep himself abreast with the current events in his country or community which are creating quite an impact on the socio-political scenario. Interviewers often post tricky question to test the general knowledge of the interviewee. All employers expect their employees to be socially aware and keep themselves updated about the current events. As a parent it remains your duty to notify your children about these possibilities. You can infact have discussion with them about the latest momentous happenings in the world and enhance his knowledge about current affairs. These discussions would not only help you to bond together but would also help his career prospects.

Challenge

> **"Challenges are what make life interesting; overcoming them is what makes life meaningful."- Joshua J. Marine**

Even eagles need challenges to soar to the heights of the azure blue sky. Similarly, your precious child who has had a relatively easy existence being protected and cosseted by you and your partner now needs some challenges to face the hard core reality of life. Before he lands his first job and jumps into the fray you can test his mettle with other types of challenges. These challenges would serve a dual purpose. On one hand they would help him to find out how to handle tough situations. On the other hand these challenges would also brush up his rusty social skills and help him to interact with people from all age groups.

Teenagers often have quite a closeted existence. They don't feel comfortable interacting with anyone apart from their peer group or family members. However, if they want to be successful in their jobs they have to learn the art of communication and interaction. So, it's up to you to challenge him to do so. You should play a vital part to challenge your teenager to discover and explore his/her interest.

The best way to do that is to challenge them to be part of the community or business world by volunteering at local charity offices or local business. Often local charities and shops employ volunteers or apprentices to work for them and give them a hand without being paid. You can encourage your adolescent child to take up to work as a volunteer or an unpaid apprentice. Even if they might not have monetary gains through this voluntary work but this type of extracurricular experiences would truly help them to discover themselves and their work potential.

This kind of exposure would also aid them in developing the much needed skills in business world like communication, leadership and interpersonal skills. As Abigail Van Burn said " **If you want children to keep their feet on the ground, put some responsibility on their shoulders."** When they meet different sorts of people through their voluntary or apprentice work they would learn how to handle them efficiently. They would learn how to tackle and tide over rough spots. Not only that these kind of experience in voluntary work can be mentioned in their resumes too. Employers often appreciate this kind of exposure and experience in their junior employees or trainees.

Evaluate

Winston Churchill had once commented **"True genius resides in the capacity for evaluation of uncertain, hazardous, and conflicting information**." As parents you can also immensely help your child to build a successful career if you provide him with an objective evaluation of his strengths and weaknesses. You can help with evaluation in two different ways.

Evaluate the Causes of their Difficulty in getting Jobs

If your child is having difficulty getting a job for whatever reason then you should be concerned. Repeated rejections and inability to secure a job after a number of interviews is infact a serious situation because this would affect his confidence level. Getting rejected and hitting a brick wall time and again may have a negative effect on his attitude and self esteem. If a pessimistic bent of mind develops in your teenager kid then that might not only impact his future job searches but that is going to permeate into other spheres of life too.

Even if it might seem like an exaggeration but it is really true that for young individuals getting a job is a reaffirmation of their self esteem and self worth. So, it is your duty to find out where your kid is going wrong in his job searches and interviews. You need to find out the crux of the problem and help him out.

After each unsuccessful interview you need to sit down with your child and make a clinical review of the interview process. You never let any judgmental or critical words creep into this objective assessment. You should merely try to hit on those weak areas which need working on. Try to find out what type of question was asked in the interview and how he responded to it. Then individually evaluate each answer that he had given and provide him with any tips and suggestions on how he can frame those answers better.

Try to conduct mock interviews by role playing as an interviewer. Try to make your kid understand that practice would make him perfect. Re-assess his resume too and if you feel that it should be more impressive then you can even rework on it too. Apart from that try to provide him with a positive support and appreciate the effort that he is putting in to find a job. With your loving support he would be able to handle rejection better and won't lose his hope of landing a good job. It is important for you to prevent him from feeling dejected and negative about his job prospects because that might have serious repercussions on his psyche at a later date.

Evaluate the Problems in Handling a Job

If your child succeeds in landing his first job then that doesn't mean that he won't need your help and support any more. You should also keenly evaluate his/her behavior and reaction after he/she starts going to the first job. Try to find out whether they are getting bogged down trying to handle school, work, sports and extracurricular activities'. People fall in three categories when it comes to handling work and school.

- Students who handle work and school with good balance.

- Students who handle school well but falter at work

- Students who handle work well but falter at school

It remains up to you to evaluate and decide whether the pressure to handle a job and school is too much for him. If he is merely cribbing because he doesn't like his schedule being bridled by the working hours or he is really experiencing a burn out.

Sometimes it might also happen that your kid might really hate being stuck in office where his colleagues are unfriendly or the work atmosphere is not congenial. You have to try to find out the real problem and help him cope with them. Try to find the tell tale signs which would tell you what he really thinks about his job. Does he say "I really hate my work", "It's really boring out there" etc? You need to evaluate the behavior and you need to provide valuable advice on organizational skills. You need to make him understand that work atmosphere need not always be congenial and he has to learn to tackle even difficult colleagues with diplomacy.

If he is not doing well in school since he started work then you might help him out a bit with his studies. You can even communicate with his teachers and get their suggestion to bring a considerable improvement in his academic life. Try to encourage him to concentrate on his school projects and home works more. You need to teach him proper time management skill which would help him to handle both work and school with proper flair. It is you who can be a beacon of light as he flails to handle his education and career.

In other words, you have to be a pillar of support during the crucial time when your offspring makes the crucial transition from academic life to work life.

CHAPTER 12

PUTTING IT ALL TOGETHER

"Give to the world the best you have, and the best will come back to you." ~ Ella Wheeler Wilcox

This chapter aims at giving a nutshell summary of all the chapters you have read so far. This would not only help to have a glimpse at the bigger picture all at once but it would also help you to revise the key points which you have patiently read in details so far. For those who have the habit of reading a book backwards, this might be a good start to get an idea about the book too!!

Chapter 1: Why We Interview and What are we looking for?

The Purpose of an Interview

The interview process is the procedure of meeting a wide array of prospective candidates and choosing, within a very short period of time, the deserving candidate for a particular position. Thus, when an interviewer takes an interview he is actually making judgments on candidates based on the facts available on their résumés as well as the interview answers and the non-verbal gestures and postures of the candidates.

Choosing the right candidate is of immense importance to an organization because a wrong candidate means loss of money, resource and time. It's quite obvious that the interviewer would be quite discerning while choosing an interview candidate and you as an interviewee need to put in your full effort to come out of the interview with flying colors.

What does the Interviewer look for in an Interviewee?

If you know what are the qualities the interviewer would be searching in you during an interview then you can prepare yourself accordingly. **FACECIA** is the acronym for **facts, attitude, confidence, experience, communication skills, interpersonal Skills and analytical Skills.** If you keep in mind these key criteria then you can ensure all round success wooing the interview.

Facts: The information you provide to your interviewer must be 100 percent true and well organized. Don't fabricate any information in your resume and try to be quite honest about the gaps in your career or employment.

Attitude: A positive and enthusiastic attitude towards the job applied for is another key criterion to woo the interviewer. Complacence is a cardinal sin for an interviewee. Your interviewer would try to find out whether you have a positive attitude and whether you are self motivated.

Confidence: Your level of confidence can often make or break your job prospects. An interviewer would never approve of a candidate who is not confident about his abilities and skills. Your level of confidence should permeate from your body postures, your gestures like your handshake and from your interview answers.

Experience: Interview success depends on the way you market your experience. If you don't have relevant experience it depends on you to underscore your other relevant skills and emphasize the fact that despite lack of experience you have it in you to succeed in the job.

Interpersonal Skills: A good employee should always be a team player and should be able to communicate with his clients and co-workers in a perfect manner. That's why the interviewer would keenly assess your interpersonal skills. It would be a prudent gesture on your part to prepare a list of examples in which you were part of a successful team effort.

Analytical skills: Your problem solving abilities and your analytic skills are of key importance during the interview. Try to find out relevant examples from your career or academic life where you had found a solution to get out a tricky situation with your rational prowess and ingenuity.

If you keep these above mentioned facts in mind then you can rest assured that you are well on your way to land your coveted job. These are the basic criterions on which your interviewer will evaluate you during those crucial rounds.

Chapter 2: Getting Started

When does the hiring process start?

Many interviewees are under false impression that the selection procedure of the prospective job candidates start from the moment they enter the interview room. This cannot be more far from the truth. The hiring process starts from the moment you hand in your resume to your employers.

Try to remember that first impressions are vital in a job scenario. Thus, you could be screened out or eliminated before you even handed in your application, if you are not well groomed or don't behave impeccably. To avoid this you should take certain measures which would guarantee that you secure your dream job.

Pre-visit the Premise and Introduce Yourself: When you pre-visit the office premise before your interview to hand in your resume, you should keep your eyes open. During your visit to the office premises of your prospective employers, you can seek out the manager and supervisor of that premises and ask them if they are hiring.

Get the Supervisor's Business card and Talk about Employment criterion: If you get acquainted with a supervisor during your visit to the office premise prior to the interview, this would help you to strike a personal touch to the interview process. You can ask a few questions to the supervisor about what the job entails and what kind of employees are they looking for. This would add some extra bits of information to the formal job description you might get.

Talk with the employees and Observe the Environment: The employees of the organization might also be able to give you valuable information about the corporate culture of the organization. The ambience of the organization especially if it is a retail outlet should provide you the key details about the organizational policies of the company.

Six Degrees of Separation: Try to find out some contacts with the organizational honchos through your friends and relatives and glean as much information about them. This would help you to assess the interviewer better and in turn prepare for the interview better.

Filling up the Application Form

Filling up the application form is a vital step in securing a good job. You should be quite cautious about certain things when you fill up the application form. These vital hints and tips are enlisted below.

Neat and Tidy Handwriting: Even if you have a scrawny handwriting, while filling our job application form, try to put in an effort to make it as neat as possible. No body would take the trouble to peruse your application form with its untidy and illegible handwriting.

Match the Application Form with your resume: The details you provide in the application form should totally correspond with your resume.

Fill up the Application form completely and correctly: Read each and every portion of the form with due care and fill up the form with accurate details. Don't leave out any portions of the form blank, search relevant information about your job experience and academic skills and insert that information.

Gaps in History and Criminal Record: Don't prevaricate about the gaps in your job history or academic history. Maximum employers tally the details in the application forms with résumé details and if any instances of prevarication happen you would be accused of duplicity of facts. The same theory applies for any law and order problem you might have faced. Don't hide them from your employers because if they get revealed later you would lose your credibility.

Salary Expectations and Availability of time: Do not put in your application wage or salary expectation which is unrealistic or out of market range. Try to be flexible and accommodating in your job timings, rigid timing restriction would limit your job chances.

Positions Applied for and Personal Interests: Try to glean information about the position you are applying for and don't just put "anything" in the section which enquires about job position. In the hobbies or personal interest section of the application form you should put some meaningful goals and hobbies in this section rather than stating that you like "watching TV."

Keep these key tips in mind while filling up the application form and you would just take a step forward towards landing your dream job.

Chapter 3: Where to Begin

What is a resume?

The next correct step that you need to take is to prepare a resume. A resume is also known as a Curriculum Vitae or CV. It is a snap-shot summary of your life till the present date. The resume is actually a marketing tool to project yourself in the best light, to your prospective employers. According to me, RESUME is the acronym for "Record of Employment Suitability and Useful Manipulation of Expertise'. I truly feel that such an expansion of the word brilliantly encapsulates its basic purpose, which is precisely to fetch employment.

To write an ideal resume you have to glean information about the common resume styles. The most common resume styles are:

Chronological Resume: The chronological resume enlists records of events or employment in a chronological order beginning with most current achievement or employment first and continues until your last employment. The advantage of this format is that, it builds credibility and shows progress and growth over time.

Functional Resume: Functional resumes lay emphasis on skills and qualifications rather than the years of experience. This is best used when you are entering the market for the first time with limited or no experience, for example, if you are a high school student, university student, or a graduate. This is also custom made for home makers or social workers who don't have relevant work experience but possess an array of skill sets.

Effective Hints for Creating a Perfect Resume:

Insert your accomplishments in your resumes not your duties. The interviewer would not merely be interested in knowing what you did in your previous jobs but he would rather know what you achieved and gave back to the organization.

Use Effective Action words like accomplished, achieved, devised conceptualized etc in your resume to draw the attention of the screener.

Avoid loose or uncomfortable phrases like "I am hard working." Or " I like people."

Highlight your personal data in ways which compliments your job interests. At times, it is your ingenuity, presence of mind or diligence, which is portrayed through a personal situation in your previous employments that is evaluated thoroughly when you get considered for a new post.

Include your non-job related experiences like voluntary work experience or teaching experiences in Sunday school within your resume.

Proof-read your resume time and again to make it flawless.

Enhance the visual appeal of the resume by printing your resume in colored papers like beige, cream or light yellow.

Choose fonts carefully so that the resume is easily legible.

Writing a resume is not enough to catch the eye of your prospective employer; you need to write a great cover letter too.

What is a Cover letter?

Cover letters are also termed as motivational letters or job application letters. Cover letters can be defined as an introductory letter that comes as an attachment to a resume or curriculum vitae.

Function of Cover letter

The cover letter essentially performs the function of a medium of communication between the applicant and the prospective employer. A Cover letter is an explanation on why you are sending your resume.

It is a specific documentation on what you are basically seeking, your objective. To put it simply, cover letters should focus on your specific skills and experiences that are most relevant to the requirements of the job in question.

Your cover letter might be sent with your resume as a response to a job posting, as a prospecting letter or in certain cases it is also sent as a networking letter to probable employers.

What should a cover letter contain?

The initial portion of your cover letter should indicate the purpose of your writing it. The middle paragraphs should spell out the details that you desire to offer to your prospective employer. In the closing paragraph of a cover letter you should mention the manner in which you would like to follow up your letter.

Cover letters and resumes compliment each other. Keep these key points in mind to write perfect resumes as well as cover letters.

Chapter 4: Interview Formats

There are various types of Interview formats, and gleaning information about these formats would help you to prepare for them better.

Individual Interview: This is perhaps the most common form of interview which is conducted by different organizations. In this sort of interview there is usually one on one communication between a single interviewee and a sole interviewer. However, in individual interviews several rounds of interview might be conducted.

Often many companies conduct Group Interview instead of individual interview. This is becoming the growing trend in the present corporate scenario.

Group Interview: This type of interview is usually attended by 5-6 candidates. This type of group interview not only saves time and money but helps to evaluate the interviewees' interpersonal skills. The candidates are usually expected to participate in a group discussion. This format of interview is quite challenging because every body remains on their toes to impress the interviewer. The key is not to be brash and bold but to be polite yet dominant among the group.

Panel Interview: A panel interview is that type of interview, where a group of interviewers take the interview of a single candidate. A panel interview is basically an evaluation of the general aptitude and attitude of the candidate. While a single interviewer speaks to the candidate, others usually keep a close watch on the body language of the candidate. So, you have to be doubly cautious about your gestures and postures in a panel interview.

Campus Interviews: As the name suggests these sorts of interviews are taken by the representatives of reputed organizations in the college campus only. This type of interview is more popular in the professional or technical field like engineering colleges or technical institutes. The whole concept of the campus interviews is largely dependent on the industry and its requirement of a specific type of human resource. A deep knowledge of the course material as well as a confident demeanor can help you succeed in a campus interview.

Behavioral Interview: The purpose of this type of interview is to find out about the inherent aptitude and competency and confidence level of the person through the past experiences and reactions the candidate has gone through. This type of interview has been quite popular since the 1970's.

Importance of Different Rounds of Interview

Most interview formats except the Campus interviews follow this generic pattern of different rounds of interview.

First Interview: The first round of interview is very crucial because first impressions often create an indelible mark on human mind. Dress up impeccably for the interview and don't get too nervous. Keep up your positive attitude and paste a bright smile on your face when you meet the interviewer. The key thing for first interviews is elaborate research. Find out detailed information about your job profile and impress the interviewer at the very first go. The interviewer would also note your body language in this first round.

Second Interview: This second round of interview means that you have crossed the initial screening round. This round of interview is much more challenging than the first round and be prepared for some tough and challenging questions.

Third Interview: This round of interview is usually conducted to test your knowledge about the organization and to see whether you would fit in with the company culture. This is often a formality to introduce the candidate to the person who takes the final decision of hiring.

Chapter 5: How to prepare for the interview?

What is phone screening?

Telephone interviews or telephonic screenings are the current norm for many employers. They especially resort to phone screening or telephonic interviews for candidates who do not reside in the same city. During a telephonic interview you have to sell yourself with your words and your voice. The purpose of such telephonic screening is to complete a quick evaluation of the candidate.

There are certain key hints and tips which you should remember to be rewarded with success in telephonic interviews. These are as follows:

Let your voice be lucid and Enthusiastic: Your voice should be clear and keen when you speak with your interviewer.

Stay tranquil and don't get over zealous: The key to come of a telephonic interview is to stay calm and composed while you iterate your points to your interviewer during your Tele-conversation.

Don't be over familiar: Even if your tone should be cordial, you should act in an over familiar manner with the employer and babble on.

Be Succinct and Factual: You shouldn't ramble while answering the interview questions on phone. The answers given during telephonic screenings should be precise and accurate.

Copy the gist of the conversation: The telephonic conversation with your interviewer might be of great help during the actual interview. So, be ready with a pen and paper and copy down the key details of your Tele-interview.

Don't eat or smoke during your telephonic interview: Telephones are sound sensitive and if you keep on munching on something then it might be irritating for the interviewer.

Preparations for an interview:

There are various fundamental aspects of preparation for an interview. Following are the key aspects in researching about your prospective employers.

Research about the Organization: Detailed Research provides you the opportunity to know about the company culture. Extensive research also helps you to find out about the company's standing in the market and the latest products or projects they have launched. You can find out about the company from the Company website, audit reports, stock reports, press releases as well as industry news.

The Day before the Interview You should Take care of certain key things:

If you follow these basic tenets then you will be fully prepared to face the toughest questions of the interviewer.

Glean information about the job details: This would help you to find out about the specific skills you need to highlight in front of the interviewer in order to impress him.

Take Additional Resume Copies and don't be late: You might need to submit one with the receptionist before the interview. This would show how prepared you are. Glean information about the route to the place where you are going for an interview and arrange for your transport. You don't want to huff and puff there at the last minute do you?

Review and Rehearse: Review the interview answers you have prepared and tally them with the job description once again. You can even conduct mock interviews to attain fluency with your interview answers. This kind of rehearsals is of immense help to attain success in interviews.

On the day of the Interview

So, now you are all set for the D-day. All you need to do now is face the interviewer with zeal and confidence. Avoid smoking and strong colognes lest you irritate the interviewer. On the day of the interview paste a bright smile on your face and be confident. Stride into the interview room and firmly shake your hands with the interviewer. Remember first impressions are often the last impressions.

Chapter 6: Answering Interview Questions

Rehearse:

As mentioned in the earlier chapters the key to succeed in an interview with flying colors is to rehearse and rehearse again. Try to find out the possible questions to be asked in the interview and rehearse with your friend and family members. This would allow you to highlight your best facets and key strengths in the least possible time through your interview answers.

Know Yourself: The best way to prepare for an interview is to make an objective judgment about your own positive and negative facets.

Use the S.W.O.T method to practice rehearsing for the interviews. S.W.OT is the acronym for

Strength

Weakness

Opportunity

Threat

Strength: One of the stock questions that an interviewer asks is about the strengths of the interviewee. To face this question with alacrity you should make an honest evaluation of your personal qualities, skills and abilities and formulate your possible interview answer based on these. Sometimes the interviewer might perplex you by asking "Why should we hire you?" These types of questions are also aimed at finding your positive qualities you should highlight qualities like ingenuity, team spirit, leadership qualities etc.

Weaknesses: The interviewer would show quite an interest about knowing your weakness. Don't give such simplistic answers as "I don't have any weaknesses". You are not supposed to be flawless. However, when you iterate about your weakness emphasize how you have taken adequate steps and measure to overcome them.

Opportunity: The interviewer might often ask you what opportunities you see for yourself. You should highlight to the interviewer what opportunities of growth you have. This may be a new vocational course you are taking or a MBA program you plan to join. You should emphasize that you are keen on growth and plan to climb up the ladder of success. Harp on the fact that you are also enthusiastic about the opportunity and exposure this particular job might provide you.

Threat: Threats and challenges are part and parcel of work life. Your interviewer thus would be keen to evaluate your trouble shooting abilities. You should provide him with real life instance where you have solved problems with your presence of mind and alacrity.

Behavioral Questions

Some Interviewers however don't ask conventional interview questions like "Tell me about your major contribution to your organization and why it was so important?"

You should remember that there are two types of behavioral questions. One type of behavioral questions deal with positive situations like "Give an example when you motivated others?" On the other hand, a negative behaviors question can ask you" Tell me of a time you failed in a project" You shouldn't get shocked with these questions and try to present a negative situation in a positive light. In other words you should detail the effort you took to save your failure, what you did to redress the situation and how you learnt from your mistake.

These types of behavioral questions are best answered with S.T.A.R method which is the acronym for Situation, Task, Action and Result.

Situation: This refers to a particular scenario or problem you might have faced in your organization. You should objectively describe this scenario in a factual manner without rambling.

Task: Then you should move on to elaborate how this particular problematic scenario had to be solved with a full proof action plan. Thus you should outline the arduous task that you had to handle.

Action: This would enlist the actions or measure you took to materialize your action plan.

Result: Your final task would be to enlist what concrete benefits you or your company achieved from your action plan.

This technique would enable you to answer the trickiest questions in a jiffy.

However after every interview your should Review or evaluate your technique so that in case you don't get this job you can work on your mistakes and put in a better effort the next time.

Chapter 7: References

It is customary to provide at least 3-4 references in a resume. However, quite surprisingly enough very few interview candidates take these references seriously. Resume references can be a grand way to market yourself too, if these references speak about you in glowing terms. However, quite often candidates get disqualified by the prospective employers because they choose the wrong references, who bad mouth about the candidates. That is why it is imperative that you chose your resume references with due care.

How should you choose your references?

While choosing your resume references you should ensure that you have informed them about the calls they might get from your prospective employers. You shouldn't provide the names of any ex-employers who fired you or with whom you had a big row. Make sure the contact numbers you have provided about your references are up to date and not old invalid ones. You should also ensure that your previous company doesn't have any organizational policy against giving references.

There are two types of resume references and you should ideally provide one of each in your resume. Usually the employers ask for the contact number and contact details. The first one is your previous or current supervisor/manager to be used as references, which are known as professional references. The second type of reference is the personal reference, where you have to provide the contact details of a person from your personal acquaintance who can vouch for your academic qualification etc. You should avoid providing the numbers of family members and relatives as personal reference.

Back ground Checks: Many organizations these days employ professional people for getting a detailed back ground check of their prospective employees. Background check involves the applicant to sign a legal document, which allows the employer to check the background of the applicant for criminal offence, credit problems, bankruptcy claims, child support issues and work history. So, if you have had these problems in the past it's always better to come clean about them to your future employers.

Chapter 8: Body Language

A first-rate interviewer will minutely assess the non-verbal communication signals which come from the gestures and emotions which your body sends. These gestures and expression would determine to a huge extent whether you are communicating positively or effectively during the interview. Thus, Non- verbal communications during an interview is of immense importance for the interviewees. Update yourself about the dos and don'ts of non verbal communication to avoid making any faux pas during your interviews.

Interview Attire: The way you dress in an interview could make or break your job prospect in many cases. Formal wear is best for attending interviews. Formal wear for men entails coordinated jacket/ suit, shirts and trousers and for women it includes suit and skirts. Avoid eye catching jewelry or accessories during an interview. If you are going for an interview in a retail outlet or a ware house, wear business casuals like button down shirts and khakis for the interview instead of formal wear.

Personal Grooming: If you are well groomed during the interview, your interviewer would always appreciate the trouble you have taken. For men a clean shaven look goes best but if you have a beard make sure it's well trimmed.

Gestures and Postures: Gestures and postures play a key role in impressing an interviewer. Make sure that your handshake with the interviewer is firm and impressive and not sweaty and limp. Avoid defensive gestures like crossing your arm and casual gestures like crossing your legs and slouching. Open gestures are always preferred over crossed ones, since they are more credulous and convivial.

Hand movements: Many interviewees during the interviews are often at a loss where to keep their hands during the entire interview rounds. Hands should ideally rest on the lap or on the arms of the chair. Don't use too much hand movements from the very beginning however, when the interview gets too animated then you can use hand movements to emphasize your points.

Facial Expressions: An interviewer usually places great impression on the facial expression of the employer because facial expressions reveal a great deal about the emotions playing through the interviewees mind. It is therefore imperative for you to manage your facial expressions during your interview and avoid showing negative emotions such as anger and bitterness. Even if an interviewer throws a question at you which you might consider rude or intrusive you should never arch your eye brows or scowl at him. Don't bite your lips if you are at a loss for words when faced with a tricky question.

Eye Movements: Eye movements also form an essential part of non verbal communication. From the moment you shake your hand with your interviewer you should try to establish direct eye contact with him because if you are shifty eyed he might stamp you as too timid or untrustworthy.

Voice and Intonation: You should use your voice to reflect your enthusiasm in your prospective job. That is why it is essential that you don't speak in a droning monotone. Use refined diction and avoid using coarse language during the interview.

You can use your non-verbal communication skills to effectively impress the interviewer and brighten your job prospects.

Chapter 9: Thirty Common Interview Questions

This chapter deals with some of the most common questions that the interviewer might ask you.

However before trying to find out the answers about these questions you must know that there are two types of questions.

Open ended question: This type of questions require a detailed elucidation from the candidate. The interviewer asks these questions to get to know the facts about the candidates' life and career elaborately. Open-ended questions usually commence with "Who, what, when, why or how". For example, "What are your strengths?

Close ended Questions: These kinds of Questions are usually answered with a "Yes" and "No". These sorts of questions are asked when the interviewer wants a definite answer without prevarication. Close-ended questions are usually constructed like this: "Have you ever fired a subordinate", "Did you ever fail in a project?" But as an interviewee you can add some other details while you answer this type of question with "Yes, but ..." or "No... however."

Some of the top questions have been enlisted below.

Tell me about yourself?

Why do you want to work for us?

Do you always make decisions on your own? When do you seek help from others?

How do you handle difficult people?

What would your previous direct reports say your strongest points are?

The other 25 questions have been discussed with hints and answers in Chapter 9 of the book. Peruse through the pages to find out how you can woo your interviewer with these suitable answers.

Chapter 10: How to Survive First 90 days in a Job

The actual test of the mettle of a candidate starts after he lands the job going through a grueling round of interviews. When you join a new organization, people would try to perceive notions and ideas about you. Thus, if you want to make your stint at your current organization a successful one then you should strive hard from the beginning to prove your merit as a valuable asset of the organization. The consummate qualities that you need to imbibe in your self to ensure over all job success are discussed in this chapter.

Positive Mental Attitude: Mastering a positive mental attitude will allow you to shape up a positive perception about you in the minds of your colleagues and bosses. Try to instill a bright and sunny persona and avoid appearing peevish. It is always a great idea to make people feel important, and appreciating people would always earn you some brownie points with them. You should also refrain from grumbling and complaining about your new work place and work environment otherwise you might be stamped as a negative and pessimistic person which would be detrimental towards your professional growth in the organization.

Goal Setting Capabilities: Starting afresh with a new job is about managing expectations and nothing makes you manage your job expectations better than setting appropriate job   goals. Try to be aware of each and every nuance of your job description and job responsibilities so that you are able to set up such common goals which would be commensurate with the expectations your reporting head might have from you. You should ensure that your goals are objective and achievable.

Observation Power: Joining a new job is always a discomfited phase but you shouldn't be speedy in judging your new company or your co-workers and take decisions for drastic change without consulting your colleagues. You should always try to observe "What" is going on your new organization and seek out "Why" those decisions are being implemented. As per your detailed observation you should chart out your decisions and behavior.

Adaptability: Adaptation to change is the key to success and survival in every sphere of life and this rule applies to your new job too. Getting a job also introduces new environment to individuals and this new environment brings major changes with it. The first 90 days in any job is a time for learning adaptations and adjustments. You need perseverance and determination to sail through the rough spots in your new organization.

Ability to take Initiatives: If you want to reach the pinnacle of success in your new occupation then you should always try to become pro-active in what you do. If you really want to take initiative and want to establish yourself as an upbeat employee then you should not always restrain yourself within your charted job responsibilities and departmental duties. However, in order to take initiative into those arenas which are new or unknown you should learn how to think and plan ahead otherwise your initiatives might just turn out to be a mere faux pas.

Team Spirit: All organizations want their employees to be true team players to ensure that optimum utilization of work resource. As a team player you must always underscore your positive attitude and team spirit. Your willingness to strive for the overall success of your team should come across to your co-workers. You have to remember that resolving conflicts in an amiable manner is the intrinsic characteristic of a great team player.

Integrity and Strength of Character: Integrity defines who you are, what your values are and how you keep your promise. An employee of true character and integrity is expected to take the responsibility of actions and clarify himself when he does something which is wrong or isn't approved of. Loss of respect is a critical situation for a new employee because earning back people's respect is quite hard thus you should never resort to unscrupulous means to get a short cut to success.

Leadership Qualities: If you want to absorb leadership qualities in yourself then you must lead by example and egg on your team members to follow your commendable work competence. You should tutor others how to solve problems and troubleshoot proficiently. There is no thumb rule that a leader has to be flawless. You should be unassuming enough to accept feed back and productive criticism positively.

If you implement these basic rules and key qualities you would be showered with success not only in the first ninety days of your new job but through out your work life.

Chapter 11: Advice to Parents

In this modern cut throat world of jobs and careers the parents should try to be parenting educators rather than simply the mother and father of the children. Thus, as parents it is your duty to support, cultivate and encourage the children to rise up and build their careers. The immense rise in the cost of living and diminishing disposable income of their guardians and parents often put additional pressure on high school, college and university students to start working early. It significantly depends on you to extend a helping hand to your kid to find his first job.

This chapter discussed how you can you help your teenager to secure his first job.

P.E.A.C.E which is the acronym for Prepare, Encourage, Advice, Challenge and Evaluate actually elaborate on the methods you should adapt to guide your offspring in his initial job searches.

Prepare: There are a wide array of ways in which you can prepare your teenage child to face the professional world. You can help him to create a perfect resume which would highlight his skills and strengths in the best possible light. Another way you can prepare your children for their future careers is by exposing them to a real-life work environment.

Advice: In your zeal to help and prepare your children for their successful careers you shouldn't mollycoddle them or stifle their individuality. Let him take the initiatives about his own career.

However, while giving advice you should be extra cautious about not hurting his morale by comparing him with his more successful peers and providing real life instances of successful careers to him.

Challenge: Challenges are what make life meaningful and interesting. The preeminent way to do that is to challenge them to be part of the community or business world by volunteering at local charity offices or local business. This type of exposure would also assist them in augmenting the much-needed skills in business world like communication, management and interpersonal skills.

Evaluate: frequent rejections and inability to secure a job after number of interviews might hamper the self confidence of your kid. That's why you should help him evaluate himself objectively after each interview and try to find out the cause of his repeated failure.

You should do this objectively without criticizing him and try to help him overcome his problems. Even after he has landed a job he might face problem balancing his work life and academic life. It remains up to you to evaluate and decide whether the pressure to handle a job and school is too much for him. You can help him handle his work pressure and academic demands by teaching him time management skills.

This book is customized to help you succeed in your career by charting you a perfect path to secure your dream job. I hope the summary of this book would help you to get a glimpse of the key topics discussed in this book. Read On...